Restoring God's Image

The Narrow Gate to Healing
and Transformation

JOHN DELGROSSO, MFT

Unless otherwise indicated, all Scripture quotations in this publication are from The New American Standard Bible, Copyright the Lockman Foundation 1960, 1962, 1963 1968, 1971, 1972, 1973, 1975, 1977.

Copyright © 2008 by John DelGrosso

All rights reserved. No part of this publication may be reproduced, stored in a retrieval system, or transmitted, in any form of by any means, electronic, mechanical, photocopying, recording, or otherwise, without prior written permission, except for brief quotations embodied in critical reviews and certain other noncommercial uses permitted by copyright law. For permission requests, please contact John DelGrosso at 626-226-7326.

ISBN-10: 144950244X
EAN-13: 9781449502447

Ordering information

www.Restoringgodsimage.com

626-226-7326

DEDICATION

This book is presented in thanks to the Lord Yeshua for His mercy, grace, and Healing in the life of His people.

I am extremely thankful to my wife Sandra, my partner and support in the struggles of life. And to my daughter Anna Lily for the time she gave up with her daddy for this project.

Special thanks to Paula Delong for her encouragements
Bill Ireland for his writing and editing talents.
And to Sally Dicken for her computer talents

ENDORSEMENT

Finally, a book that goes beyond *information* to *transformation*. **Restoring God's Image** is not another Christian version of a self-help book that offers insight into the why's of our problems, pains and addictions. Instead, by taking seriously scriptural teachings on sin, forgiveness and healing it leads the reader down the path to genuine renewal. John DelGrosso does not simplistically declare "Jesus is the answer," he shows *how* God heals our hurts. If you or someone you love needs to get on the pathway to restoration, this book is for you.

Dr. Jim Reeve
Senior Pastor
Faith Community Church

Restoring God's Image

TABLE OF CONTENTS

Help Me, Lord!	1
The Big Picture	9
Our New Identity	23
Nine Misconceptions	35
Pain Is a Good Thing!	47
Lies We Believe: Our False Reality	59
Strongholds	71
Resentment	81
Vows	89
Judgment	97
Vain Imaginations	105
Victim	115
The Narrow Gate	123
Confession	133
Receiving the Truth	141
Putting it all Together	149
Moving Forward	159
Index	165

CHAPTER ONE

Help Me, Lord!

*God is our refuge and our strength,
A very present help in trouble.* (PSALM 46:1)

This is not another self-help book. If you have picked it up believing that change will be easy, you will be disappointed. Rather than promising easy transformation through new behaviors, its purpose is to help you struggle through the agonizing pain of *true* transformation.

Christians often speak of *crucifying the flesh*. Galatians 5:24-25 states, "And they that are Christ's have crucified the flesh with the affections and lusts." But how many of us really embrace this, and welcome the experience of pain when it occurs? Many churches and self-help books are trying to help us *avoid* pain, rather than seeing it as a catalyst for transformation, a necessary experience in our journey to freedom in Christ. Paul speaks of losing everything "that I may know Him and the power of His resurrection and the fellowship of his sufferings." Clearly, pain is part of the package.

In my years as a Christian therapist, I have worked to bring healing to God's people through the transforming power of Christ, and nothing else. In 1 John 1:7 we read that "If we walk in the light as He is in the light, we have fellowship with one another, and the blood of Jesus Christ His Son cleanses us from all sin." That's what I want people to experience. It's a work that Jesus began on the cross, and continues as He helps each of us carry our own cross.

People typically come to me desperate for change, as they struggle with addictions, fear, anxiety, and loneliness. They all realize that something is wrong. They're not experiencing the freedom they've heard about in sermons and songs that they sincerely believed in. When they do find freedom it's temporary, and then their problems overwhelm them again. They've learned to think positive, set boundaries, manage anger and follow steps, but in the end find themselves cheated. Why?

The answer goes back to the deep spiritual truths revealed in the book of Genesis: We have been duped and deceived by the enemy of our souls. Does this apply even to Christians? Jesus told us that times would eventually get so bad that if it were possible, even the elect would be deceived (Matthew 24:23-25). The writer of Hebrews warns his Christian readers of the dangers of being "hardened by the deceitfulness of sin" (Hebrews 3:13). Unfortunately, even Christians can be deceived.

Because we in America have so much blessing, we believe that whatever we're doing must be adequate and right. But this is false. Years of absorbing the tenets of psychology and its inaccurate conclusions have led us down a destructive path. Even as we follow this errant way, we pray for God to bless our pursuits. How futile! As Jesus said, the way to destruction is wide.

But there is a path that leads to life. It is narrow, as Jesus said, but He guarantees our success as we walk in it; He's already shown us the way. In fact, Jesus Himself *is* the way: "I am the way, the truth, and the life. No one comes to the Father except through Me" (John 14:6). He does not abandon us to our own abilities. By His power within us, He enables us to accomplish more than we can ask or imagine. Reading this book will not help you to become better, but *will* help you decrease, as Christ in you increases. You'll learn to do this through the scriptures. True Christian counseling should be the way of the cross—the way to life—the way of God.

Most Christians would agree that the Bible is true, and following its precepts is the only way to live. But then, they routinely go outside the scriptures to find truth and healing. We trust our hearts and lives to men and women who know nothing of the cross or the blood of Christ. We learn principles conceived by men outside the Body of Christ, and expect them to produce lasting spiritual results. Worse, we use and embrace new age principles and language. It is not that studying these principles is always worthless, but we cannot trust them for transformation.

Our goal is to become conformed to the image of Christ, as Romans 8:29 says: "For those God foreknew he also predestined to be conformed to the likeness of his Son…" How can a non-Christian author help us do this when he does not accept the divinity of Jesus? How many of our most accepted principles are fostered by teachers who don't even believe God exists? What fellowship can light have with darkness? (2 Corinthians 6:14).

Christian therapists are often trained by non-believers, and apply unchristian principles to achieve spiritual change. How can this be so with the body of Christ? How can we believe that any good thing can come out of the world? In the face of this contradiction, we often take these unregenerate principles and cover them with a thin veneer of scripture, hoping that will confer legitimacy. But it can't. Teaching men to overcome their problems through self-effort and personal strength will never pass the test of scripture. Such efforts will be burnt up as wood, hay and stubble, as the scripture says.

So is psychology completely powerless to change people? No. God has extended His mercy to all. Just as God uses the medical field for people inside and outside of His kingdom, He can use psychology too. But medicine with all of its advances cannot prevent the ultimate death of its recipients. So psychology cannot defend people from the power of deception that comes through sin. Lasting transformation is only accomplished through God Himself. As Romans 8:28 tells us, God will use all things (even that which is not good) for good for those who love Him, and who are called according to His purpose. He also uses hardship to chasten and teach us. But we must not be seduced by attractive programs that ignore God's truth. As Paul tells us, the message of the cross is "foolishness" to those who are perishing. But "the foolishness of God is wiser than men" (I Corinthians 1:18-25). He offends the mind to reveal the heart.

As you read on, consider what *God* would have you do. Be willing to enter the pain you've been avoiding for so long, and allow Christ to walk into it with you. That is how He will bring His truth to you — not the false truth of self-effort. Walk with Him through the narrow gate that leads to life.

I'VE BEEN THROUGH COUNSELING BEFORE!

Jim and Sue came to me at the end of their rope. They were in danger of losing their relationship, their hope and their faith. They had been referred to me precisely because they wanted counsel from someone who understood their faith in Christ. After the first session, Sue spoke up: "We've been to counselors before, but this is different. It's not what we expected. What you're saying is easy to understand, because it's based on scripture. Most of all, you asked us to bring everything to Christ."

This shouldn't have been so surprising. As Christians, we have the Holy Spirit living in us, so we are able to discern things spiritually. When we experience truth, it is Christ in us speaking, and the Holy Spirit gives a resounding *yes*! We receive the truth in our minds, but the understanding and hope come from the Spirit within us. That's our inheritance as new creatures, born again of God. "If any man is in Christ, he is a **new creature;** the old things passed away; behold, new things have **come**" (2 Corinthians 5:17).

People who have been in therapy often assure me they've worked through everything in their past. Then when the old issues resurface, they say, "I thought I'd dealt with that already!" Usually, they've only come to a partial understanding of their past events, and have never dealt with the deep issues that prevent their healing. We will explain several of these principles in the pages that follow: resentment, vows, and strongholds.

Healing requires an encounter with the living God, and the simple yet life-changing principles established in scripture. Scripture is essential for the life of God's people. If that is so, we must make certain that the things we depend on for change and healing are supported by God's word. We shouldn't entrust our lives and relationships to unscriptural ideas.

Here's a good illustration: Gina and her husband Ed came to me for counseling after several Marriage Encounters and classes on communication. They also had seen at least two therapists over the previous eight years.

Things would go better for a while, but then the fighting would begin again. Whenever Ed had to work late or leave on a business trip, Gina would feel abandoned. It seemed he was putting everything else in his life before her. In previous counseling sessions, Gina had taken the bold step of telling Ed how she felt. Eventually, she realized that she had believed a lie, and was able to tell herself so — sometimes. But then the old feelings would overwhelm her, and her mind would return to the painful refrain: "He doesn't care for me."

Ed loved his wife dearly, but when she accused him of *not* loving her, he withdrew. Through counseling he learned to communicate his feelings. Still, Gina would cry when she felt abandoned, and this made him angry. He couldn't seem to shake the pattern.

Their previous therapist told them they needed to learn to set boundaries with each other.
But the more boundaries they set, the further apart they felt. The more they tried to protect themselves from hurt feelings, the more angry they became, and the more they blamed each other. Another therapist told Gina that she should think about divorcing her husband, since he evidently didn't care about her feelings. If he did, he wouldn't leave town so often for his work. If he *really* loved her, he would get a new job!

Neither therapist ever asked them what they believed *God* wanted for their marriage.

After a few sessions, Gina was able to see that she had been harboring resentment towards Ed for the entirety of their marriage. When they were newlyweds, he would often leave her to party with his friends. She came to believe that she didn't matter to him. But as a good wife, and afraid of losing him, she didn't say anything. As the years went by, her pain became overwhelming. They eventually became Christians, and Ed stopped his partying ways. But Gina's pain didn't go away.

They tried every avenue they could find to improve their relationship. But none of the therapy, classes or communication seminars ever dealt with the strongholds which were the root of their problems. They needed a scriptural remedy.

During one session, we discovered the origin of Gina's feelings of abandonment. It was a lie that had been programmed into her as a young girl. Her workaholic parents spent long hours away from her and left her with many different caretakers, some of whom abused her physically and sexually. From then on, she believed that no one cared for her. No wonder Ed's behavior caused her such pain! This was a raw wound, and he was rubbing salt in it.

In cases like this, the lie must not only be identified, but the victim must be transformed through the application of God's truth. This is the psychology of Scripture – the *true* study of the soul! Gina thought she had forgiven Ed — several times. But she had never dealt scripturally with the *unforgiveness* in her heart. She had never been taught to confess it as sin. In fact, she had never even heard a sermon on it, in eight years as a Christian.

Gina and Ed are just two examples of hurting Christians. Are you one? Or do you meet hurting people every day? If you're alive and breathing, you surely do. Just look around during your next church service. If you reach out your hand you will probably touch someone who is hurting. You'll probably see a man who is involved in pornography, or having an affair. You'll probably see someone with a secret eating disorder, or a shopping compulsion. The statistics for Christians caught in these snares are staggering. Divorce rates for Christians are comparable to non-believers. The percentage of teens involved in sex is similarly discouraging. But God does provide a way out.

As we noted, Jesus exhorts us to "Enter by the narrow gate" (Matthew 7:13). And it's essential to remember, He *is* that gate. He is the way out of our destruction and despair. Any other way is deception.

I've heard countless Christians confide their inadequacy. "Everyone thinks that I have it all together," they'll say. "I'm so ashamed!" Maybe you've said something similar yourself. What is it you're ashamed of? That you're in sin? Of course you are! You are in the flesh. But there is good news for those of us in Christ: "Therefore, there is now no condemnation for those who are in Christ Jesus" (Romans 8:1).

As you read on, you'll learn why we all experience pain, what it leads to, and how to find God's solution. We'll begin with God, and ultimately end with God—the *big picture* that He wants us to see. In-between is the miracle of Christ, and His challenge to us as believers. I pray that you will be not only challenged, but comforted in your journey. Remember, God comforts the disturbed, and disturbs the comfortable!

Let's move forward.

CHAPTER TWO

The Big Picture

But I am afraid that, as the serpent deceived Eve by his craftiness, your minds will be led astray from the simplicity and purity of devotion to Christ. (2 CORINTHIANS 11:3)

As we see from the story of Eve in Genesis, deception has been a part of the human experience from the beginning. The gospel is about dispelling that deception. The Christian life could be thought of as a journey from deception to truth. And as Jesus said, when we know the truth it will set us free. The transformation God promises in the Bible includes our spiritual and emotional healing. Jesus signified how important healing was in God's plan by healing people physically everywhere he went. How much more important our *inward* healing must be to Him! This healing is such an integral part of our transformation that this book will use *healing* and *transformation* virtually interchangeably.

God has provided a scriptural plan for healing that He intends for every Christian. But to grasp it we need to see the *big picture*, which begins with Adam and Eve, reaches its climax with the life and death of Christ, and culminates in the restoration of God's people by the Holy Spirit. It's critical that we see this larger plan, because it affects not just the way we approach healing, but our entire understanding of it. Sadly, most Christians have completely missed the big picture. This is our greatest tragedy!

CREATED IN GOD'S IMAGE

Scripture tells us that God created Adam and Eve on the sixth day. Even though you've probably heard this story a million times, there's something really interesting here: God created them in *His image* (Genesis 1:27). When a child is born, we typically hear parents exclaim, "He (or she) looks just like me!" We can imagine God exulting the same way when he looked on His new creatures — just like any good and loving daddy. We can assume that Adam and Eve knew they bore God's image.

God placed Adam and Eve in the Garden of Eden, which in Hebrew means *garden of delight*. What a delightful experience this must have been for Adam and Eve! Not only were they created in the image of God their Father; but they walked in the cool of the day with the Almighty Himself. He was their magnificent delight. *He* is what made the garden so delightful.

After establishing Adam and Eve in the garden of delight, God blessed them and gave them their purpose: "Be fruitful, and multiply, and refill the earth, and subdue it; and rule over the fish of the sea, and over the birds of the sky, and over every living thing that moves on the earth" (Genesis 1:28). In His first words to Adam and Eve, God directed them to *take dominion* over the creation. They were also to *listen* to the voice of God and be completely *dependent* on Him. This applied not just to them, but to the whole human race that would "fill the earth" after Adam and Eve began being fruitful and multiplying!
God's original design was for us to take dominion over the rest of creation and have authority over the earth. But something went terribly wrong.

THE IMAGE LOST

In the garden of delight, God provided everything Adam and Eve needed, giving them one simple rule: In the middle of the garden, He had placed two very special trees, different from the others: the tree of life, and the tree of the knowledge of good and evil. God told them not to eat the fruit from the tree of the knowledge of good and evil. Pretty simple instructions, right?

Interestingly, at that time, the serpent was just one of the creatures over which Adam and Eve were to rule. They bore the image of God and were thus above Satan in authority and in stature. They had the authority and ability to reject his gambit. God even warned them ahead of time what the temptation would be when He gave His instructions. God knew how crafty Satan was (Genesis 3:1), and allowed him to live in the garden anyway. So, man was not yet under the power of sin, but sin was present in the person of the serpent. And because sin existed, so could the pain that is sin's result.

Scripture doesn't tell us how long it took Satan to deceive Eve. We can assume that it took awhile. Eventually, he convinced her that she and Adam were not really like God: "For God knows that in the day you eat, you will be Like God, knowing good and evil." Satan lied to Eve just as he lies to us. He implied that she needed to be something other than what God had made her. The lie she believed — that she and Adam were incomplete — brought her pain. The serpent undermined Eve's confidence in what God had said — that they must not eat the forbidden fruit, or they would die. Eve misquoted this command, and the enemy was able to use her mistake to his crafty advantage. He sowed doubt in Eve's heart, and as with all of us, it caused confusion and emotional pain.

> Satan lied to Eve, and that lie inflicted emotional pain.

It's a grim testimony to Satan's craftiness that he was able to deceive Eve, who had been created in God's image. There was no lie in her, but he succeeded in planting one. How much more can he manipulate us, who are born into a legacy of sin and deception! Eve's experience should also warn us that even after we have been healed, we're susceptible to Satan's deception. We must continually watch and depend on God.

Eve, feeling the emotional pain of the serpent's lies, had a critical choice to make. She could take her pain to God, confess the deception (lie), and ask God to tell her the truth; or she could try to fix the problem on her own. We can only assume, based on her unwise decision, that the deception was overpowering and the emotional pain unbearable. Under the weight of these two influences, Eve chose to take action. She tried to rid herself of the pain of the lie by eating the forbidden fruit. She could be like God now. The truth, of course, was that she was *already* like God. Both she and Adam were created in God's image.

The apostle Paul states that Eve first was deceived, and then she transgressed (1 Timothy 2:14). In other words, Satan lied to her, and then she found the pain of the lie so unbearable that she sinned in her efforts to remove it. She really began to believe and perceive that she and Adam were missing something — they were not like God. That one single lie was not only deceptive, but powerful, and very effective. It changed her perception of herself and Adam so much that she not only disobeyed, but made the critical mistake of not going to God. Had she taken her pain and doubt to Him, He could have told her the truth.

Through this single instance of deception and disobedience, we start to see a very clear pattern. First, Satan lies to us. The lie causes us emotional pain. We try to remove the pain of the lie through our sinful nature, just as Adam and Eve did. They sought immediate pleasure — sin —rather than trusting God to take away their pain. In their mistake, this single act of disobedience, we see a pattern that recurs in our lives today.

The word *obey* means to *listen attentively*. Eve did not listen attentively to God, and of course, Adam didn't either. We're all familiar with the results. If we think we're better than them, we are mistaken! We are no more obedient than they were on that fateful day. Like them, we do not bring our pain to God. And Satan's lies are just as powerful and effective on us; they affect our perception of ourselves, others, and yes, even God. Like them, we try to overcome the pain of the lie through our own efforts, without God. And we fail miserably!

What happened after Adam and Eve sinned? In the garden, naked and ashamed, they hid from God. But He, in His infinite and abiding love, came after them! He found them hiding in their sin and shame, and immediately clothed them. He covered their nakedness. This profound expression of love by God is a glimpse of what Jesus does for us later on the cross.

Eve was deceived and then she transgressed (sinned).
Eve sinned to deal with the pain of the lie.

IN MAN'S IMAGE

Adam and Eve were created in God's image, but through the fall, *mankind lost that image.* In Genesis, we learn that Adam and Eve had three sons: Cain, Abel, and Seth. The story of Cain and Abel is a wrenching illustration of just how far mankind had fallen. Cain and Abel evidently had some kind of relationship with God, which involved the offering of sacrifices. Abel was a shepherd, so his offering was an animal. He must have understood somehow the atoning sacrifice that God had given to his parents through the blood of an animal. Cain, on the other hand, brought God an offering of crops from the field. If we remember what happened at the fall, man was consigned to work and till the ground, which had been cursed. Cain brought God a cursed offering! He brought what he thought was good; Abel brought what *God* said was good. Abel came to God on His terms. Cain came to God on Cain's own terms. This is an apt illustration of the way we must seek healing: on God's terms, not ours. We must deal with our sin and deception in the way God says is acceptable, not man's way.

> We need to pursue healing in the way that God says is acceptable, Not in the way man says is acceptable.

Immediately following the story of Cain and Abel, a monumental reversal occurs with the birth of Seth. "Adam ... became the father of a son in his own likeness, according to his image, and named him Seth"(Genesis 5:3). The implication is that Seth bore the image of Adam — fallen man — rather than God. Most of us believe we were created in the image of God, but Scripture tells another story. Yes, Adam and Eve were created in God's image. Like them, we were never meant to live outside of God, but to live and move and have our being in communion with Him. But according to the scriptures, after the fall mankind bore the image of his fallen ancestor Adam. We *lost* the image of God!

As to our spiritual parentage, Jesus didn't mince words. As he spoke to the religious leaders of his day, he said, "You are of your father the Devil, and you want to do the desires of your father" (John 8:44). Satan gained authority over Adam and Eve when he deceived them in the garden. Scripture refers to him as "the God of this world," and like the Pharisees of Jesus' day, we have all followed his desires.

Through Adam and Eve's disobedience, death entered the world. Man would forever be under the power of sin, until …

GOD'S IMAGE RESTORED

The battle that took place in the garden between Satan, Adam and Eve was repeated many years later in the wilderness between Satan and Jesus. Scripture describes Christ as "the last Adam" (1 Corinthians 15:45-48). Immediately after His baptism, Jesus was driven into the wilderness for forty days where He was tempted by Satan. Satan tried to deceive Him just as he had deceived Adam and Eve. Adam and Eve met Satan in the garden; Jesus met him in the desert. Adam and Eve sinned to overcome the deception. Jesus, living in a fallen world, *never* sinned to overcome the deception. Jesus never succumbed to the craftiness of Satan. Instead, He overcame the deception with truth, took authority over Satan, and provided us with an example of perfect listening (obedience) to God. This man Jesus, who never sinned, gave Satan the answer Eve should have spoken in the garden: "Man does not live by bread alone, but by every word that proceeds from the mouth of God" (Luke 4:4). Like us, Jesus faced real temptation, and He had to overcome it as a man, not using his power as God. He confronted temptation as Adam did (Philippians 2:8).

> Christ destroyed the power of sin and deception.

After overcoming Satan's deception in the wilderness, Jesus humbled himself and became obedient, listening attentively to God, to the point of death—death on the cross! There, He made a spectacle of principalities and powers, completely destroying the deception of Satan and the power of sin. Satan succeeded in deceiving Eve, but Jesus overcame the deception. His cross became a tree of life for us. So who is the liar? Satan. And who is the Truth? Jesus. Deception and sin that entered the world with the fall, and Jesus overcame them both.

But something even greater happened.

After the Lord's resurrection and ascension, He sent the Holy Spirit as promised. Jesus tells us that as His sheep, we hear His voice (John 10:27). As born-again believers, we are new creatures in Christ (2 Corinthians 5:17), with God's image restored. Jesus Christ, who overcame sin and deception and took authority over the enemy, now lives inside us. So, we too have the same authority.

Paul confirms this truth in Romans: "Even so consider yourselves dead to sin ..." Our purpose now, as new creatures, is to overcome the enemy's deception in our lives. We have been justified, but need to be renewed and healed daily. Paul puts it this way: "...Lay aside the old self, which is being corrupted according to the lusts of deceit, and that you be renewed in the spirit of your mind, and put on the new self, which in the likeness of God has been created in righteousness and holiness of the truth" (Ephesians 4:22-24). As Paul notes, those lusts are deceitful. And it is the deceitful lies of the enemy — lies we believe about ourselves — that cause the pain in our lives.

Even though Jesus paid the price for our sin, most of us haven't been "transformed by the renewing of our minds." The enemy still lies to us, and we're often inclined to believe him. We live in deception. But with Christ in us, we have the opportunity to take each one of those lies to Him, and hear Him speak the truth. That is how healing happens.

There's a time for healing, and then there's a time for vigorous action. We have a battle to fight, and it's not for the timid. Paul writes about "tearing down strongholds" (2 Corinthians 10:3-6). In this battle, we must take captives: "... Taking every thought captive to the obedience of Christ." Like Joshua, we're called to wage war. The battle takes place in our minds, and we must fight it every day.

The big picture is that Adam and Eve, because of being deceived, lost the image of God through sin. Christ, who overcame the deception of the enemy, made a spectacle of the enemy and destroyed the power of sin. Through the new birth, we gain the image of God back into our lives.

THE LAST ADAM

Adam and Eve's decision to disobey God had lasting effects on every one of us. When Adam fell, we all fell with him (Romans 5:12-21; 1 Corinthians 15:20-28, 45). Paul refers to Jesus as the "last Adam" (1 Corinthians 15:45). A few verses later, He calls Him "the second man." The first Adam failed the test, after being tempted and deceived. God, in His love, gave us a second chance at redemption — His only Son, Jesus, the last Adam.

There is another distinction between these two men: "The first man is from the earth, earthy; the second man is from heaven" (1 Corinthians 15:47). God created Adam in His image, but from the dust of the ground. Christ is "the image of the invisible God" (Colossians 1:15), whose origin is heaven itself. This last Adam is the One through whom God created all things (John 1:1-3; Colossians 1:15-20; Hebrews 1:2). The first Adam disobeyed; the last Adam obeyed to the point of death. The first Adam brought death; the last Adam brought eternal life. The first Adam brought condemnation; the last Adam brought justification. Christ, the last Adam, overcame Satan and redeemed a new race.

It is in Christ, "the image of the invisible God," that we also regain God's image. Where Adam tragically lost that image, Christ, the last Adam, restored it to us. As Paul writes, "For as in Adam all die, so in Christ all will be made alive" (1 Corinthians 15:22).

> Christ, the last Adam, restored the image of God to us.

As the one sin by the first man (Adam) condemned mankind, the one righteous act by Jesus Christ set mankind free and gave us eternal life. And as Paul gloriously affirms, "There is therefore now no condemnation for those who are in Christ Jesus" (Romans 8:1). We're now free to walk as children of God, led by His Spirit.

SEEING GOD'S PLAN

Why is it so important to see the big picture? We must understand that God has a plan for us. And it's an amazing plan: God is conforming us to the likeness of Christ Himself. We must approach everything, including healing, in the context of this big picture. We see His intentions in the original creation, when He instructed Adam and Eve to rule over the earth. Through Christ, we recapture that destiny.

> In Christ, we have authority over the things of the earth.

It's important to note that Satan failed to deceive Jesus when he met Him in the desert. That victory gives us hope. Without the Spirit of Christ in us, Satan *will* deceive us as he did Eve. But as born-again, spiritual men and women, we can prevail as Christ did. Jesus overcame Satan and destroyed his works. Now, Christ living in us destroys the works of Satan in us. And what are those works? The work of the enemy is and always was deception. Jesus summed it up well: "Whenever he speaks a lie, he speaks from his own nature; for he is a liar, and the father of lies" (John 8:44). But Jesus is the truth, and came to destroy the works of the devil. Through His Spirit in us, the deception is lifted. That's the power of God!

We must remember these truths, so that in suffering we'll see God using our circumstances to conform us into the image of Christ. Paul, who knew about suffering firsthand, modeled a good attitude for us: "Now I rejoice in my sufferings for your sake, and in my flesh I do my share on behalf of His body (which is the church) in filling up that which is lacking in Christ's afflictions (Colossians 1:24). Jesus is continuing to live His life through us destroying the deception in our flesh. This eternal drama between deception and truth, Satan and God, continues in us. .

Jesus, for the reward set before Him, endured the cross. We, for the reward set before us, endure the struggle of overcoming deception in our lives. But we must always remember Paul's words: "For I consider that the sufferings of this present time are not worthy to be compared with the glory that is to be revealed to us" (Romans 8:18). Christ encountered the enemy, endured and overcame. When we encounter the enemy and his deceptions, we too can endure through Christ, and overcome.

The last enemy Jesus overcame was death. So, even death is not an obstacle for us in Christ. It is a reality for our flesh, but as the scripture says, "...When this perishable will have put on the imperishable, and this mortal will have put on immortality, then will come about the saying that is written, 'O death, where is your victory? O death, where is your sting?'" (1 Corinthians 15:54-55).

> God uses our pain and suffering to conform us into the image and likeness of Christ.

Seeing the big picture, we begin to take on our new identity in Christ. But certain questions are inevitable: What role does sin play in our lives? And why do we still have emotional pain?

Our sin is a result of the deception placed on us from birth. Our pain comes from not being in communion with God. We now must overcome the sin and deception in our lives by following God's scriptural plan for healing—not some program devised by fallen man. We have the Spirit in us, and there is no sin or lie in Christ. Therefore, in our spirits, there is no sin or lie. This is who we are in Christ. But, as the apostle Paul states, our minds must be renewed. Sin is destroyed, but we must still be transformed. The reality of Christ must reach the untransformed parts of us — what the Bible refers to as our flesh.

HOW TO APPROACH HEALING

God always intended for us to exist wholly in Him. Anything outside of Him is false, and sin. Yet, even as Spirit-filled people we indulge our fallen flesh by seeking the knowledge of good and evil. We memorize scripture, believing that we can change ourselves by increasing our knowledge. We're still trying to discern right versus wrong; trying to fix ourselves!

> We need to pursue healing through Christ, the tree of life.

I imagine that Adam and Eve found refuge under the tree of life in the garden. Perhaps that was even where they encountered God in the cool of the day. Why? Because in the New Testament, Jesus says, "I am the way, the truth, and the life" (John 14:6). But something happened when they ate the forbidden fruit. They began to understand the difference between good and evil. Because of this, God removed them from the garden.

So what does this knowledge have to do with the way we approach life and healing? Since the fall, we're all reduced to trying to be better people on our own. When we experience pain or hardship, we try to overcome it through our own merit and strength. We've lost the knowledge of God's unconditional love. We live according to right *and wrong,* rather than in relationship with God. Most of our laws and rules—even in the church—are based on this concept of right and wrong; good and bad.

The New Testament says, "For all who are being led by the Spirit of God, these are sons of God" (Romans 8:14). We are no longer left to discerning good versus evil. That knowledge is what separated us from God!

Most people live by trying to figure out what is right on their own. They seek to understand evil and good, rather than listening to the voice of God. This is where Satan gains entry and deceives us. Just like Adam and Eve, we try to find something to take care of our pain. We hear Satan's lies, and instead of going to God in our pain and asking Him to tell us the truth, we resort to sin. Then, naked and ashamed, we hide from God.

As He revealed in his instructions to Adam and Eve, God always intended for us to rule over His earth, in union with Him. Like them, we were meant to be His vessels.

SUMMARY

God wants every Christian to be healed

Healing is not optional! God is very intent on healing the deception in our minds and the deceit in our hearts. Every one of us was born into sin (Romans 3:10); and according to scripture (Romans 12:2), our minds need to be renewed. This can only occur through the scriptural methods God provides. This critical process of renewing our minds brings transformation. As Christians born again by the Holy Spirit, each of us has God's image restored to us. However, our flesh needs to be conformed into the image and likeness of Christ. Our minds are still under the deception of the enemy. We must crucify our flesh daily and learn how to renew our minds, tearing down strongholds as the scripture says.

We must pursue healing God's way

We need to seek our healing in accordance with scripture, allowing God to transform us and restore His image. This type of spiritual healing is not available to the unregenerate person, as Paul says: "But a natural man does not accept the things of the Spirit of God; for they are foolishness to him, and he cannot understand them, because they are spiritually appraised" (1 Corinthians 2:14). We must pursue healing God's way, in accordance with the scriptures, and depend completely on God for the Truth.

We need to be healed *daily*

We must ask God to search our hearts every day. Paul says, "For if while we were reconciled to God through the death of his Son, much more, having been reconciled, we shall be saved by His life." (Romans 5:10). The word translated "saved" here also means *healed.* The Greek word is *sozo,* and has the additional meanings of "make whole, heal, or be whole." The passage implies an ongoing process. We need continual healing, because we're continually vulnerable to lies.

The Bible describes Satan as the *deceiver*. Near the end of the book of Revelation, an angel throws him into the abyss, "so that he should not deceive the nations any longer" (Revelation 19:3). In II Thessalonians, Paul speaks of a "deluding influence" or a "strong delusion" that will characterize the last days. And in Romans he pronounces a verdict on all mankind, "... Their foolish heart was darkened" (Romans 1:21). But Christians are also vulnerable to deception, as Jesus noted in Matthew 24:24. He described false leaders who would "... mislead, if possible, even the elect." We must take every thought captive to the obedience of Christ (2 Corinthians 10:3-5) and allow God (not man) to renew our minds.

To be healed, we must overcome the sin and deception in our lives

Healing for the Christian involves identifying the deception and sin in us. Jesus took our sin and paid for it, but we are still deceived in our flesh. We must allow the indwelling presence of Christ to transform us radically. Jesus often equated *sozo* (healing) with forgiveness of sins, confession of faith, and peace. There is a battle going on between deception and truth in this world. Unfortunately, because we don't understand God's scriptural plan for healing, we are still trying to be healed according to the ways of unregenerate man, who uses sin to deal with the deception in his life. As regenerate men and women, we are to allow the Spirit of God dwelling inside of us to overcome the deception and sin in our lives. Just as Adam and Eve were to overcome the deception of the enemy, our purpose is to destroy the works of Satan in our lives and in the lives of those around us. It's critical that we understand that *we cannot change ourselves.* We cannot conform ourselves into the image and likeness of God. We have the image of God restored to us in Christ, but now God's plan for us is to be conformed into the image of His son. We cannot accomplish this without Christ!

We must ask God to show us the truth

Healing for the Christian must involve dialoging with God on a daily basis. Why is this so hard for us? You could say it's in our genes. Adam and Eve did not go to God when they were deceived by Satan, and their tragedy passed down to us. They thought they could handle it on their own, and we have been deceived into believing the same thing. We must talk with God regarding the deception and sin that are in us, and hear Him speak the truth to us. Then, we are set free!

We must depend completely on Christ for our healing

Yes, we were always meant to live in total dependence, communion, and fellowship with God. We need to stop settling for partial truths. Psychological principles alone may provide insight into our beliefs and traumatic life events, but can never transform us. Satan deceived Adam and Eve with partial truths about God and themselves, and that campaign continues today. God's way of healing is established in the scriptures. We now have Christ in us to tell us the Truth. Healing cannot take place until we depend wholly on Him. No one is exempt.

CHAPTER THREE

Our New Identity

Therefore if any man is in Christ, he is a new creature.
(2 CORINTHIANS 5:17)

In a famous passage, Jesus told Nicodemus, "You must be born again." When Nicodemus expressed bewilderment, Jesus explained, "That which is born of the flesh is flesh; and that which is born of the Spirit is spirit." He went on to chastise Nicodemus for not understanding the scriptures. This new birth was the *goal* of the scriptures. How could Nicodemus, as a teacher of Israel, not know that?

But Nicodemus raised a pertinent question when he asked, "How can a man be born when he is old?" He might as well have asked, "How can we accomplish what God wants by natural means?" The point is, we can't. Having been born into sin, we are utterly, hopelessly bound in darkness. Our best efforts can only produce death. This has been the state of all mankind since the fall. Only by faith in Christ can we have any hope of escaping this death sentence.

Jesus came to destroy the deception of the enemy in the lives of those that would hear Him. After His death and resurrection, He told His followers they would soon receive power from on high. They experienced the new birth Jesus spoke to Nicodemus about. God restored His image in those who believed. It was the beginning of His new creation.

Something wonderful and spectacular happens when we are born again. Christ himself enters our hopelessly corrupted flesh through the Holy Spirit, bringing life to our dead souls. By simply believing, we are transformed into new creatures, very different from what we were before. With the Spirit of God living in us, we have become a higher order of being—higher not only than unregenerate man, but higher also than the angels and demons. God Himself lives in us! As John testifies, "Greater is He who is in you than he who is in the world" (1 John 4:4).

Why is this important? Because it means that now, through the indwelling Christ, we have authority over the lower forms of being. This was God's original intent with Adam and Eve: "And God blessed them; and God said to them, 'Be fruitful and multiply, and fill the earth, and subdue it, and rule over the fish of the sea, and over the birds of the sky, and over every living thing that moves on the earth.'" (Genesis 1:28). Of course, one of those living things was the serpent. When they failed to take dominion over him, they lost the image of God and became earthly beings devoid of Spirit.

As Christians, we are new creatures being conformed to the image of Christ. He began this process in us when we were born again, and continues it daily through the renewing of our minds. As Paul puts it, "And if Christ is in you, though the body is dead because of sin, yet the spirit is alive because of righteousness." That renewal will be complete when God changes our bodies: "But if the Spirit of Him who raised Jesus from the dead dwells in you, He who raised Christ Jesus from the dead will also give life to your mortal bodies through His Spirit who indwells you" (Romans 8:10-11). He elaborated on this to the Corinthians, "...We shall all be changed, in a moment, in the twinkling of an eye ..." (1 Corinthians 15:51-52). And as he told the Thessalonians, "...Thus we shall always be with the Lord" (1 Thessalonians 4:17). That is our destination.

People I counsel will often defend their sinful behavior, saying, "Well, I'm only human," or "Everybody does those things!" I explain to them that as Christians, we're a new type of being; part of Christ Himself. The Bible describes us as His *body,* and also His *bride.* As a wife is one with her husband, so we are one with Christ.

The Bible calls us *new creatures.* What are the implications of that? Let's examine what this new creature is like. First of all, the new creature is totally righteous. He knows no sin or condemnation. She is holy, complete, united with God. The new creature hears God's voice, lives in God's love by faith, is seated in heavenly places with Christ, and cannot be deceived.

Why is it so important that we know our new identity? More particularly, how can that knowledge transform and heal us? Our enemy is constantly lying to us about who we are in Christ, just as he did to Eve. He deceived her into thinking that she and Adam needed to be something other than what God had made them. He now does the same with us, through our sinful nature, telling us we are not who God says we are. We are not loved, not good enough, not wanted, not clean, not worthy. Yes, we continue to struggle with sin. But in the new creatures that we are, victory is an accomplished fact. God is in us, fighting the good fight on our behalf.

Even as new creatures, we still must deal with our fallen nature, corrupted by sin, bound by the devil's deception. But that is not what God sees. He does not recognize the old, fallen creatures we were before. To Him, our new identity is forever complete. In Christ we are always and ever new creatures.

But doesn't the scripture tell us, "If we claim we have not sinned, we make Him out to be a liar?" (I John 1:10). Indeed, this does describe our old nature, and simply points out our need for forgiveness and transformation. If we confess our sins, John says, God is faithful to forgive us and cleanse us (our flesh) from unrighteousness. In the new creature, there *is* no unrighteousness. The deception we experience exists in our old nature, our un-renewed and untransformed minds, and provokes us to act in the old ways. As John says, Jesus is continually cleansing the sins we commit in our old nature.

In Romans 7, Paul describes how the power of sin compels us to do things we don't want to. Where does this sin reside? In our new nature? No, it is in the old fleshly nature, fraught with deception. But Paul gives us the hope of the ages, as there is now "no condemnation for those who are in Christ Jesus, because through Christ Jesus the law of the Spirit of life set me free from the law of sin and death" (Romans 8:1). This is the great, powerful good news of the gospel. Even though we live in a body of sin, we are no longer sinners. We are saints of God imbued with the very righteousness of God Himself.

Every time I consider this I'm filled with awe. This reality alone is joy unspeakable. His atoning work blotted out my sin, dark and profound as it was, and now continues to erase it as He completes His will in me. God is *continually* setting us free, renewing our minds, transforming us into His image.

As we approach God for healing, it is extremely important to know who we are in Christ. This enables us to distinguish clearly between the old and new natures. At a given moment, we may be confused as to which one we are living in. This will lead us to erroneous decisions, as we trust our emotions rather than the conviction of the Holy Spirit. Healing comes when we realize who we are through the restoration of God's image. For the Christian, transformation is healing.

Jeannie was an 18 year-old college student struggling against peer pressure. She simply wanted, as most young people do, to be liked. She had already experienced a few romantic relationships, but none of them was very healthy. In the end, she always felt used, abandoned, and hurt. She had recently become a Christian, and began attending a Christian group for young adults. She felt this would be pleasing to God. It was also important to her to please her parents; after all, they were paying for her education and had high expectations. But like many college students, she found herself doing more socializing than studying. She began failing her classes. As we talked, she described how helpless she felt. She was wracked with guilt, unable to do what she knew was right; and convinced that God was angry with her.

Jeannie needed to know who she really is in Christ. And she needed to hear God tell it to her. No human words, however well-intentioned, would do the job. I began to explain to Jeannie about her new identity, trusting God to reveal it to her heart. I told her she had been justified (Romans 5:1), and had received a new life in Christ. Through the indwelling Spirit of God, she now had a new identity. This new creature, I told Jeannie, does not sin. She is one with the Holy Spirit, who does not and cannot sin. She should consider herself, as Romans 6:11 says, *dead* to sin.

I also explained that when she sins, it is the old nature acting. She is justified, but now needs to be saved continually (Romans 5:9). As we often point out, the word "saved" (Greek: *sozo*) in this context also means *be healed*. What do we need to be healed from? From the sin and deception that is in our old nature. God's purpose for Jeannie—and us—is to transform her mind *and* body. She is struggling with this flesh, the old nature. This is where she struggles with what to do or not do. But this is not who she really is. She has already and forever been justified, her sin no longer counted against her. The blood of Jesus covers it all (Hebrews 8:12). Nothing can separate her from God's love, which is in Christ Jesus. (Romans 8:39). In fact, Jesus loves her in the same way that God the Father loves Jesus (John 15:9). Incredible!

Jeannie had been deceived into believing that she was not who she really is in Christ. Her mind needed to be renewed. Her experience had taught her that she was unloved. But this is not true in God. We prayed that God would reveal His truth to her. She felt God telling her that she was, indeed, forgiven. We then began to address the lies that Jeannie had embraced: that she was unloved, abandoned, used and helpless. Her sin was no longer a source of condemnation, but an indicator of areas where the light of God's truth hadn't reached. She needed simply to confess her sin, and allow God to wash over those areas of deception with the truth. As James 1:14 tells us, we sin because we're *enticed*. That word also means *deceived*. Jeannie had been deceived. She needed, like all of us, to listen to God and obey Him. But if she failed to do that, her remedy was simply to confess her sin, and God would forgive her. This was good news indeed.

THE BENEFITS OF OUR NEW IDENTITY:

1. *Sin can work for our benefit.*

If Jesus paid for our sin and God does not condemn us for it, why are we still grappling with it? Couldn't God have removed us completely from our old nature? Of course, but for His own reasons He chose not to. Apparently, He has some lessons for us to learn. As Paul says, "We have this treasure in earthen vessels, that the surpassing greatness of the power may be of God, and not from ourselves" (2 Corinthians 4:7). In other words, God wants us—and everyone else—to know that any goodness we exhibit is not our own. It comes from Him. And we must depend on Him for our healing and transformation. This is precisely what Adam and Eve failed to do.

In the familiar verse from Romans, Paul writes, "And we know that God causes all things to work together for good to those who love God, to those who are called according to His purpose" (Romans 8:28). Do *all things* include even our sin? Actually, sin can have a beneficial function for the believer. It tells us that something is wrong. In fact, the only way we recognize our sin is through the revelation of the Holy Spirit. Unregenerate man is unaware of his sin, and scoffs at the very idea. But for us, sin points out the areas of deception, where we're still living in our old nature. As we'll discuss later, sin is also part of the stronghold we erect to protect ourselves from pain. The remedy is to *confess* our sin. That allows God to cleanse those unredeemed areas of our lives.

Since we have this new freedom, are we therefore free to continue to sin? As Paul says emphatically in Romans 6:2, the answer is *no*. Sin is inconsistent with our new identity. But we can regard sin as a signpost that lets us know we're deceived. As heirs of God through Jesus, we can overcome the deception, just as He did. We can walk as Jesus walked, destroying the work of the deceiver.

2. *We can now hear and obey God.*

The scriptures tell us that if we love God, we will obey Him. But, most of us have a warped concept of what this means. The world teaches us to focus on our own performance. We only have value if we perform well. Thus, it becomes very important that we do the *right thing*. But in Christ this is totally irrelevant. *He* has made us pleasing to God. *He* has made us right. So we seek to obey Him, not to gain His approval but to show our love.

We obey by listening, and following His word. Paul speaks of "taking every thought captive to the obedience of Christ" (2 Corinthians 10:5). The word "obedience" here means to *listen attentively*. To really do this, we must understand how powerful the Word of God is. According to the scriptures, God created the universe by *speaking*. To put it mildly, when God speaks, things happen. This is the same God who calls us, speaking healing and transformation into our hearts. Obviously, it is very important that we hear what He's saying. As Jesus said, "My sheep hear my voice" (John 10:27).

But that's where our problem lies: Because of our sin, we can't hear God. We're told to be doers of the word, not just hearers. But we must hear first! Thus, a major part of our healing is regaining the ability to hear God. Then, the very power that created the universe creates change in us. Jesus modeled this process Himself: "I do nothing on my own initiative, but I speak these things as the Father taught Me" (John 8:28). He now lives in us, enabling us to hear the Father as He did. We have the privilege of bringing our thoughts to God, and hearing Him respond. Then we fulfill the scripture, "For all who are being led by God, these are sons of God" (Romans 8:14).

The Bible makes clear that we are not to depend on our own intellect in solving life's problems (Proverbs 3:5). Rather, we must depend completely on God for guidance. This is not just for a few super-spiritual believers. As John said, "The anointing which you received from Him abides in you, and you have no need for anyone to teach you" (1 John 2:27). Jesus said the Holy Spirit "will teach you all things" (John 14:26). Without the Holy Spirit, we are completely helpless. He reveals our hearts, shows us truth, and gives us direction. We must allow Him to test all our actions, thoughts and beliefs. As God's children we always have the ability to hear Him. And as we will discover, He provides specific ways for us to hear Him and receive His healing.

3. *God is working His will in us*

Because of the fall, we have all learned to *do* for ourselves, rather allowing God to do His work in us.

Sadly, this virus affects Christians too. Paul, after urging us to "work out" our own salvation, reminds us that "It is God who is at work in you, both to will and to work for His good pleasure" (Philippians 2:13). That brings up a profound question: Is God's will ever thwarted? Perhaps He needs our help to accomplish what He wants. That misguided notion is behind many of our attempts to *become* something—better people, or better Christians. But as Jesus asked, "Which of you by being anxious can add a single cubit to his height?" (Matthew 6:27). We can only become what He wants us to be. Clearly, He has a different calling for each of us. But for all, His will is that we yield ourselves fully to Him, giving up our natural efforts to achieve spirituality. The scriptures say that God watches over His word to perform it. And He has placed each of us in His body, so He can express Himself in different ways. We are not to compare ourselves to others.

God's will is more than something He decides. It is a powerful, mysterious force that is part of His very person. And it is unstoppable. We can't know it on our own, but He works it in us through the Holy Spirit, doing things we could never accomplish on our own. This was the power at work in the disciples at Pentecost, when Peter was transformed from a traitor into a fearless preacher of the truth. A few days earlier, the disciples were oblivious to God's will, even though they had witnessed countless miracles at Jesus' side. He told them it was better for them that He should go away, so He could send the Holy Spirit. Then, God would work His will *in* them. That day, they discovered what He was talking about.

4. *We have victory over Satan*

Some people in the church emphasize spiritual warfare, devoting much time and energy to Satan and his demons. The Bible tells us these forces exist; in fact, they are the very source of the deception many of us grapple with. But the danger is that by focusing on them, we'll avoid the real work of change. This misplaced emphasis can also lead to an unscriptural fear of the demonic. As we've noted before, "Greater is He who is you than he who is in the world" (1 John 4:4). With the God of the ages living in us, we're higher than these demonic forces. Moreover, they can't touch the image of God which He has restored in us. Satan can only enter where deception exists. By rooting out the deception in our lives, we disrupt his influence. As John reminds us, "The Son of God appeared for this purpose, that He might destroy the works of the devil" (1 John 3: 8). He accomplished this on the cross, overcoming death itself. Satan still roars like a lion, but with Christ in us, we can chase him away!

5. *All things work together for our good*

Many couples come to me convinced that their marriage cannot be saved. They've endured hardship, mistreatment, or adultery, and can't seem to forgive each other. In some cases, they have to face the reality that a spouse might *continue* doing hurtful things. How can this be a good thing? Why should anyone tolerate it? I'm afraid that in the midst of these struggles, we miss the meaning of suffering and redemption. In these moments we have the privilege of manifesting God's unconditional, agape love. This is never easy, comfortable, or painless. We'll inevitably find ourselves being crucified. But we'll also learn to love as God loves. When we stand in these difficult, impossible situations God uses them for our benefit. But, we must stand.

I've walked with many believers through dark nights where victory seemed impossible. Sometimes, they had to accept that their circumstances might *never* change. And the world was always there too, delivering its seductive message: Quit. Give up. Save yourself. But when these believers learned to sit, listen and talk with God, they experienced His presence. And that makes everything different. God manifests His will *through* our suffering.

6. *We have God's agape love*

Sadly, most of us misunderstand the nature of love. We've all heard people say, "I've fallen out of love," or "I know my mother loves me." We long for a love that doesn't change. But only God's agape love is constant. Human beings, even Christians, do not love continually. We know this is true from experience. We've all been mistreated by people who insisted they loved us. Human love depends on feeling, and that's why it is unreliable. A person involved in an illicit affair may feel great. A Christian man may force his wife to have sex, insisting that he's acting out of love. But God's agape love is never present when we're sinning against someone.

Question any newlywed couple and you'll hear how much they "love" each other. Probe a little further and you'll hear words like, "He makes me feel great!" or "I've never known this feeling before!" But as soon as that spouse does something that produces a bad feeling, which is inevitable, love collapses. God wants to teach us a new kind of love—one that always seeks the other's good, always cares, never gives up, and never fails. This love overcomes evil, destroys strongholds, and forgives the unforgivable. We can only love this way if we are new creatures, bearing God's image. He teaches it to us through hardship.

7. *We have access to spiritual weapons*

Paul describes his life as an apostle this way: "…Commending ourselves as servants of God…by the weapons of righteousness for the right hand and the left" (2 Corinthians 4:4,7). What are these *weapons of righteousness*, that he carries in each hand? He gives us a clue further on: "For the weapons of our warfare are not of the flesh, but divinely powerful for the destruction of fortresses. We are destroying speculations and every lofty thing raised up against the knowledge of God, and we are taking every thought captive to the obedience of Christ" (2 Corinthians 10:4-5). These weapons pull down strongholds of sin, unbelief and deception. Christ Himself, the righteous one, gives them to us. They include things that don't seem like weapons, such as prayer, confession, listening to God, and invoking the blood of the Jesus. But these tools can accomplish great things.

8. We can counter deception with truth

The Bible gives a bleak diagnosis of our natural condition: "The mind set on the flesh is hostile toward God; for it does not subject itself to the law of God, for it is not even able to do so" (Romans 8:7). This hostility to God shows especially in the way we respond to the gospel: "For the word of the cross is to those who are perishing foolishness" (1 Corinthians 1:18). This explains the scorn nonbelievers commonly feel toward Christianity. But according to the scriptures, we aren't just inclined to reject God's message; in ourselves, we can't even understand it: "But a natural man does not accept the things of the Spirit of God; for they are foolishness to him and he cannot understand them, because they are spiritually appraised" (1 Corinthians 2:14). Before we are born again and have God's image restored, His message makes no sense to us.

In that light, it's all the more marvelous and miraculous that we can now hear God's truth—and comprehend it. The verdict on mankind expressed in Romans is that we "exchanged the truth of God for a lie" (Romans 1:25). As new creatures, we can exchange the lie for truth.

9. Christ lives in us in, whatever our circumstances

It's worth examining again a passage we've quoted earlier: "If we say that we have no sin, we are deceiving ourselves, and the truth is not in us. If we confess our sins, He is faithful and righteous to forgive us our sins and to cleanse us from all unrighteousness" (1 John1:8-9). John describes a process whereby Jesus is continually taking our sins, so we are never condemned. What does this mean? It means, as Romans 8:38-39 makes gloriously clear, that nothing can separate us from God's love. No matter what depths we sink to, God is there with us. We cannot hide from Him.

David understood this well:

"Where can I go from They Spirit?
Or where can I flee from Thy presence?
If I ascend to heaven, Thou art there;
If I make my bed in Sheol, behold, Thou art there.
If I take the wings of the dawn,
If I dwell in the remotest part of the sea,
Even there Thy hand will lead me,
And Thy right hand will lay hold of me."
(Psalm 139:7-10)

As Paul writes again in Romans 8:32, "He who did not spare His own Son, but delivered Him up for us all, how will He not also with Him freely give us all things?" If Jesus paid the price for our sin, then He will remain with us. As He said, "I will never desert you, nor will I ever forsake you" (Hebrews 13:5).

This is vividly illustrated in the life of Linda, a woman who spent years living on the streets addicted to alcohol and drugs. Many churches observed her sinful behavior and summarily rejected her. They saw her inability to overcome her addictions and concluded that she must not be a faithful Christian. Indeed, Linda entered numerous recovery programs, and would seem to do better for awhile. But in the end, she always returned to her destructive ways.

What few people could see was the pain behind her actions. Linda, like many addicts, was a victim of childhood sexual abuse. She had been a little girl once, who trusted people and expected good things to happen. Instead, the people who should have protected her betrayed, exploited and tormented her. She had no one to comfort her or put things in perspective. No one taught her how to forgive, to hear the voice of God, or to receive His healing. This trauma led her to believe lies about herself, other people and God. When the pain of those lies became unbearable, she turned to anything that might dull it for awhile. Other people saw her behavior, but couldn't hear the cry of her heart.

But God heard, and He saw. After Linda's death, family members found her journal. It revealed her deep love for Christ, and a heartbreaking awareness of his daily mercies. She recounted the numerous times God had rescued her during her grim life on the streets. At times, it seemed miraculous. In one instance, Linda entered a public restroom and was followed by an attacker. He was in the midst of assaulting her when a voice over a loudspeaker scared him away. But an inspection afterward revealed no speaker in the room.

Another incident happened while she was struggling in a drug treatment program in Los Angeles. Linda had retreated to a nearby park to think and watch the pigeons. One of them seemed sick, and Linda's sympathy was aroused. She approached the little bird and picked it up. That's when she noticed the little cross someone had tied around its neck. Meaningless? Maybe to some people. To Linda, it was another small sign of God's presence.

Christ was always with her. He never left, even while she struggled with sin and life on the streets. This is the depth of His love and mercy towards His children. As the prodigal son was never far from his father's heart, so Linda was never far from God. In this life, she suffered from her own addictions and the cruel acts of others. In God's presence, she has a seat of honor. The enemy had tried to destroy her from her childhood on. In the end, he could not wrench her from God's hands or destroy the testimony of Jesus in her heart.

CHAPTER FOUR

Nine Misconceptions

"He himself bore our sins in His body on the cross, so that we might die to sin and live to righteousness; for by His wounds you were healed. For you were continually straying like sheep, but now you have returned to the Shepherd and guardian of your souls.
(1 PETER 2:24-25)

There are countless misconceptions among Christians about what it means to be healed, and how it is accomplished. As Christians desiring truth, we need to identify these false notions and understand how they prevent us from experiencing the healing and transformation God wants for us.

Imagine driving on a country road at night, and coming to a crossroads. Since you're in unfamiliar territory, you're not sure which road to take. You have no map or GPS; you're at the mercy of what you can see, which isn't much. Suddenly, you notice a signpost with signs pointing this way and that, but they're ambiguous and confusing. If someone from the area were present, you could ask for directions, but there's not a soul in sight. You've lost all sense of direction and can't seem to regain your bearings. Even though you're a sophisticated adult, you begin to feel panic. You turn right and start down a road that seems like your best bet. After a few miles, you change your mind and double back. Soon, you're back where you started, facing the same choice. You try another road, but now you have another worry—you're running low on gas.

This is what a lot of Christians are like as they approach the subject of inner healing. We know we're in trouble, and we have to make choices. But the right way isn't clear. We worry that we'll run out of resources and be stranded, with no hope of finding our way home. The detours we take are like the broad road Jesus described, which leads to destruction. They never lead us to the truth. Worse, following them wastes precious time and resources, leaving us helpless, hopeless, and disillusioned. If we persist, it can cost us our lives.

But what if we've already made that wrong turn, and are feeling disillusioned and hopeless? If that is your case, take heart. Along that dark highway of the soul, there is a signpost that is not confusing or misleading. It leads to life. Before we get to it, we need to point out some of the misleading road signs that people follow. Through my therapy practice and personal experiences, I've identified nine common misconceptions about healing. Perhaps you'll recognize some of them.

1. *I'm a Christian, I don't need healing*

This is perhaps the greatest of all misconceptions!. Many Christians believe that our salvation *is* our healing, and Christ's work in our life is complete the moment we receive Him into our hearts. But the Apostle Paul emphatically states that we are to be transformed by the renewing of our minds (Romans 12:2). Renewed from what? If we are Christians, what is in our minds that needs to be renewed? Paul alludes to the ongoing work of Christ's life in us—beyond our initial experience of salvation: "For if while we were enemies, we were reconciled to God through the death of His Son, much more, having been reconciled, we shall be saved by His life" (Romans 5: 10). These scriptures speak to our need for continuing transformation. As the psalmist says, "Your mercies are new every morning." If our transformation were instantaneous and complete, we wouldn't need new mercy every day! As we've noted, God is conforming us into His image (Romans 8:29), and the image of God, lost at the fall (Genesis 5:3), is restored to us in our spirits when we receive Christ. However, our minds must be renewed for that conforming to take place.

2. *I can change myself*

Walk into any Christian book store today, and you will see hundreds of Christian self-help books. While some of them do touch on the power of

Christ to heal and transform us, there's a lack of clear, simple, Bible-based instruction on how to find release from emotional pain.

We're taught that knowledge is power; that by learning more we can make ourselves better—we can heal ourselves. This is false. To paraphrase Paul's admonition to the Galatians, why is it that we begin in the Spirit, as new creations in Christ, and then continue in the strength of our own will? Is it because God is not powerful enough to change us? Jesus asked, "Which of you by being anxious can add a single cubit to his height?" (Matthew 5:27). If He were speaking to us today, he might say, "Which of you can change who you are by reading a self-help book?" Why do we think that we have power to change this flesh, sinful as it is? As Paul writes, "We have this treasure in earthen vessels, that the surpassing greatness of the power may be of God and not from ourselves" (2 Corinthians 4:7).

We become Christians, and then imagine that we can continue to maturity without Christ. We try to subdue the flesh and its sinful ways through our own will, using fallen man's techniques. But our nature is stubborn, as Paul notes: "For the good that I wish I do not do; but I practice the very evil that I do not wish (Romans 7:19). He identifies the source of our problem as the power of sin. He reaches an unavoidable conclusion that every honest human can identify with: "Wretched man that I am! Who will set me free from the body of this death?" (Romans 7:24). Then he gives us the hope that we seek: "Thanks be to God through Jesus Christ our Lord!" (Romans 7:25).

Any healing methods, psychological or religious, that do not depend solely on Christ are doomed to fail. Only Christ in us can conform us to His image.

3. *I just need Jesus*

Since each of us has a personal relationship with God, we're often tempted to believe that we don't need other people. This is a great lie from the enemy that separates us from our brothers and sisters, and contradicts the Word of God itself. The Scriptures never state that we "just need Jesus" and no one else. True, Christ is the Great Physician, the ultimate source for all healing. But, I see another motivation in people who make this statement.

They're responding to painful interactions in their past, which led them to make vows of self-protection. They are simply fulfilling their vows! We will discuss these vows in greater depth later.

There is a purpose in our pain and suffering. To find it, we must follow God's prescription. First, we need to share our pain with others. God created us to have fellowship with Him—*and* one another. Our healing begins when we confess our sins to one another (Luke 17:3-4; Ephesians 4:32; and Colossians 3:13). We are also instructed that there is wisdom in a multitude of counselors (Proverbs 11:14, 15:22, 24:6). Many Christians only take part in large meetings, and miss out on the intimate fellowship of a small gathering or one-on-one relationship. But this is the setting where we can tell our stories and allow others to hear our hearts—and then experience healing.

Some of us believe that fellowship only takes place on Sunday mornings, or during weekly Bible studies. We think these superficial interactions are all there is. Worse, we think we have to maintain a Christian image to impress other people. So, when we're in pain we hide and protect ourselves from our fellow believers, afraid that if we expose ourselves they'll judge us harshly. Thus, we miss Christ. We must have safe places to reveal our sin and the painful lies we've embraced, where we won't be criticized but rather restored in love.

Since most of our deep emotional wounding occurred in past relationships, our healing must take place in *current* relationships with our brothers and sisters. And we may find that our brother or sister struggles with the same things. When we hide and protect ourselves, no one hears our struggle, no one can share our pain, but most importantly, no one witnesses the power of Christ to heal and transform us.

After Jesus' resurrection, He breathed on His disciples and said, "Receive the Holy Spirit" (John 20:22). Then He said something remarkable: "If you forgive the sins of any, their sins have been forgiven them; if you retain the sins of any, they have been retained." (John 20:23). Each of us as believers has authority in Christ. As the Apostle Paul emphasized, we need one another, and the gifts of the Body of Christ. There is a mystery that His body displays when it functions in unity. Jesus said that where two or more are gathered, there He is in the midst of them (Matthew 18:20). It should not surprise us that true inner healing most often takes place in the context of relational, Christ-centered community.

4. *I can learn to say and do the right things*

We take it for granted that we can read books that will teach us how to say and do the right things. We're convinced we can change our behavior, shift our thinking and correct our habits on our own. Such efforts may work, but only in the short term. When they don't last we find ourselves back where we started, wondering why our efforts—conceived out of a pure desire to change—did not work.

You might ask, "But isn't it important to change what I say or do, especially if it's causing problems in my marriage, family, or other relationships?" Yes, absolutely! But how this change comes about is more important than the change itself. It must be a result of the transforming work of Christ in us. Then, it is permanent and irreversible, and we no longer have to work.

I've seen countless couples and individuals try to learn how to say and do the right thing. Or, they'll try to get their partners to respond in a different manner: "What do I have to do to get my husband to take responsibility for his actions?" "What do I have to do to feel loved in this marriage?" "What do I do now that my wife is seeing another man?" It's all about seeking ways to modify *behavior*. These questions are relevant, especially if we're seeking solutions in our marriages, family, or other relationships. But they miss the truth of scriptural teaching. As Paul makes clear in the passage quoted earlier, the very things we want to do, we can't. When we seek the *right thing* to do or say, we have reverted to the knowledge of good and evil (as we describe in Chapter 2, The Big Picture).

God wants to show us a "better way," as He says at the end of 1 Corinthians 12—the way of love. Then we will understand that *right* is not necessarily loving. In all our efforts, we're usually trying to limit the pain inside, or between us and someone else. But if we learn to say or do the right thing without being transformed first in our minds and hearts, we will find the effort fruitless.

Jesus was able to do what He did because there was no lie in Him. He embodied perfectly the will of God. We can only accomplish what we need to *do* as we become what we need to *be*. We need to be renewed each day. Acting as if we are healed is not the same as being healed. That is why unless change occurs in our hearts, we become like the Pharisees whom Jesus described as "whitewashed sepulchers." Paul prays that "you would be changed in your inner man." That means a long, often painful process. Perhaps that is why Paul had to spend so many years in Arabia, or Moses in the desert or David in caves when he was running from Saul. When hardship occurs in our lives, we can surrender and let it change us, or return to what we have all learned in the flesh: trying to do and say what is right.

During counseling sessions, people often ask "What should I do." I always respond with a question: "What is God telling you to do?" When Jesus was confronted by some hostile leaders, he said, "...He who sent Me is with Me; He has not left Me alone, for I always do the things that are pleasing to Him" (John 8:29). He preferred the will of God over what might have *seemed* right. And it got Him in trouble. But He retained the most important thing: fellowship with His Father. He refused to save himself, to set up boundaries, or to call down the legions of angels at his disposal. He could have smitten His enemies as the apostles suggested. But He knew that listening to His Father was the only true way to live life, and it is the only true way for us to be healed as children of God. We'll discuss this further in the chapters to come.

5. *I don't need to look at my past*

We all seek freedom in the present, but few of us want to look at our past. Like the present, our past has many unredeemed places of pain and sin—places where Satan and his angels have gained a foothold, and then erected a stronghold. We want to believe that if we just forget about the past, we can move forward. But we can't. Many Christians take the scripture "forgetting what is behind" (Philippians 3:12-14) out of context to believe that we are to ignore the past. This would work well if we had all followed the instructions of Scripture growing up, and spent our entire lives confessing our sinful acts to the Lord. If this were the case, we would not have any strongholds of darkness in our minds. But that is not the case. We were all born into sin, and most of us continued in sin well into our lives.

Clients and friends often ask me, "Why do I have to look at the past?" My reply is always the same. "Everything is the past, isn't it " That usually draws a puzzled response, and I continue: "What you just asked me a minute ago is in the past." In fact, what you just read is now in the past! If looking at the past were forbidden or a waste of time, why are we instructed in Scripture to go to one another when we've been offended? (Matthew 18:15). Why are we told to confess our *sins*—events that happened in the past? (1 John 1:9). What is the Apostle Paul referring to when he says we need to be transformed by the renewing of our minds (Romans 12:2)? What do we need to be transformed from? Isn't it the false beliefs and sinful actions of the past which have taken over our lives and led to the formation of strongholds in our minds? When we become Christians, God no longer remembers our sin, but our flesh still needs constant transformation from the lies and influences of the past. And that past can extend all the way back to conception. We will explain this more in Chapter 6, The Lies We Believe.

6. *I just need to study Scripture*

Studying scripture is a worthy pursuit, one that I've engaged in for many years. God definitely speaks to us through the scriptures, but He also has other ways of speaking to us. Didn't Jesus say, "My sheep hear my voice"? (John 10:27). Doesn't John state that we have the Holy Spirit and don't need men to teach us (John 14:25-26)? What did John mean by this? Of course, the gift of teaching is an important ministry in the Body of Christ, but cannot itself produce the healing we need. The Pharisees knew scripture backwards and forwards, yet their hearts were hard. They were blind and under the law. In a similar way, unless we deal with the deception in us, even our understanding and application of scripture can be compromised.

We all know Christians who don't behave like Christians. We generally accept that God is bringing us all to maturity, but that also implies that immaturity still exists. Part of that maturing process is learning to hear God directly. While we expect Him to speak through His word, we must never forget that our relationship to Him is multi-leveled. It isn't that knowledge of the scriptures is bad. But it can become an idol, and we can lose the message of the Gospel—the power of Christ Himself in us to heal and transform.

It is also important to recognize that studying scripture is not the same as applying it to our lives, especially in the way God tells us to. I can know it is important to love. But if I don't remove the roadblocks to loving that exist in my heart, my knowledge is wasted.

In the area of healing, we must learn to apply the scriptures in the way that He tells us. Of course, it's easier to use scripture to puff ourselves up. We think that if we know enough, we will be closer to God, or more mature. But most of us have never been taught to apply God's word to identify the strongholds of darkness in our lives, and then allow Him to transform them.

7. *I just need more insight.*

We tend to believe that if we look at our problems long enough, analyze them, talk about them, and try to learn from them, we will eventually experience healing and transformation. Many of my clients come to me after prior counseling experiences, and insist that healing has already occurred. This may or may not be true, but often they're simply accepting what the previous counselors have said. They truly believe that they have completed the healing process in one area or another, because they've been taught that intellectual insight is the same as real spiritual change. It is not.

While there is a place for insight in the process of healing, and certainly a place to talk about our pain and experiences, there is also a time when intellectual insight must give way to truth as revealed by Christ. Often we relegate our need for truth to scripture reading, or the acquisition of knowledge about ourselves, as if that were the completed work. This is not the case when it comes to healing of our minds and hearts, or when it comes to being mature Christians and doers of the word.

This insistence on analyzing and fixing things in our heads is the very obstacle that prevents us from experiencing healing. In fact, we need outside intervention precisely because we as humans are limited by our meager temporal experiences. As we gain insight about ourselves we experience what we think is freedom, but this is an illusion. We find true freedom only when our minds are renewed. Insight is not renewal—it's just more information! Sometimes that information does more harm than good. All of us have areas that we hide even from ourselves. This is a defense mechanism, intended to limit our pain. When we discover this hidden information without achieving resolution, we only cause ourselves more problems It certainly is good to see that we are in need, but that's not the same as having our needs met.

If I believe that my new insight is all the change I need, I'll stop seeking and become paralyzed. Some of my reactions may shift in accordance with this new insight, but this is not scriptural healing.

George is a good example. As a young man, he constantly experienced friction in his relationships with other men, especially authority figures like pastors or bosses. Eventually he realized that this was a response to the abuse he'd suffered as a child at the hands of his father. Because of this trauma, he approached all similar relationships with fear and mistrust. He embarked on a program of behavior modification to change his responses, but it was based entirely on will power. Of course, it never got off the ground. He learned to control his outward responses, but inside the old feelings were still seething. The strongholds of darkness were still in place.

George didn't need insight. He needed to be healed. Until that took place, all he could do was trade one means of self-protection for another. True *spiritual* insight transcends our natural, rational experiences. It comes from the Spirit of God, and leads to real healing.

Does this mean that we should never seek insight through secular counseling or other activities? No. God uses every way possible to reveal His Truth to us. But to really transform us, insight must be followed by repentance and hearing the truth of God.

8. *I just need to let it go.*

This has become a popular phrase. I often hear it when I counsel clients or friends struggling to forgive someone who mistreated or abused them: "I just need to let go of the pain, and move on with my life."

The truth is, we can't "let go" of our pain.

In fact, most people have a wrong understanding of emotional pain and its purpose in our lives. Most of what we describe as *letting go* is really our desire to suppress, deny, and run from our pain. We try to forget things, instead of seeking forgiveness and repentance. If we *could* simply let things go, why would Christians struggle as much as nonbelievers with emotional pain, anxiety and depression?

9. *I'm supposed to suffer*

While we do partake in the sufferings of Christ, we must understand what this really means so we don't needlessly endure emotional pain, anxiety, depression, and other ailments the Lord may want to heal. The disease in our bodies may be linked to the deception (lies and strongholds) in our minds and the sin in our flesh. Once we see these strongholds, we can begin, with Christ, to tear them down using the instructions of Scripture.

God uses suffering to chasten us. The term *chasten* here means to *send hardship,* not to intentionally inflict pain for its own sake. This hardship reveals what is in us—what we believe. Most often, it reveals the lies that support our thinking. God may bring physical and emotional suffering to us so we'll draw closer to Him. God is willing to remove our suffering, but He sometimes will not remove it if we remain bound by the lies and sin that cause it. He will work in us to allow suffering to have its perfect work. God, being sovereign, chooses what experiences we must walk through. He knows how to conform us to His image.

"We rejoice in our sufferings, knowing that suffering produces endurance, and endurance produces character, and character produces hope, and hope does not disappoint us, because God's love has been poured into our hearts through the Holy Spirit which has been given to us" (Romans 5:3-5).

Most of us are familiar with religious ascetics who actually seek suffering, sometimes deliberately inflicting physical pain on themselves. Even evangelical believers will punish themselves with long fasts or sleepless nights of prayer, all in an effort to please God. Believing this will help them conquer the sinful flesh, they identify with Paul's comment, "I buffet my body." But how can fleshly activities conquer the flesh? Clearly, this is not what the Bible means by "sharing the sufferings of Christ." This mindset flows from a skewed picture of what God requires. Any technique that diminishes the finished work of Christ has missed God's purpose.

Clearly, we all experience suffering in this life, including nonbelievers. But there is a certain frame of mind that gravitates to suffering, expects it, and even relishes it. People may derive a false sense of pleasure from the belief that they're "suffering for God." They may even place themselves in risky situations to provoke the pain they crave. Most tragically, they miss the healing work that God would do in them.

Others wallow in a victim mentality, feeling sorry for themselves and thus avoiding the struggle necessary to change. They justify it all with the unquestioned belief that "I'm supposed to suffer. There's nothing I can do about it." Such self-pity is inconsistent with the hope the scriptures provide. These actions, too, are driven by strongholds in our minds. They leave us weak, helpless and unchanged.

SUMMARY

God wants to heal us. To grasp this plan and purpose, we must dispel our misconceptions about healing. Even after we receive healing, we may go back to our old sinful habits, and find ourselves doing the very things that prevented us from being healed in the first place. By identifying and refuting these misconceptions, we can come to know the truth—God's powerful plan for healing in our lives.

CHAPTER FIVE

Pain Is a Good Thing!

And we know that God causes all things to work together for good to those who love God, to those who are called according to His purpose. (ROMANS 8:28)

Are you in pain? Are you struggling? Are you wondering if anything good could result from what you're experiencing? The answer is a resounding *yes*! The scriptures provide great encouragement for saints who are suffering. Under God's providence, all things—even our sorrows, trials and persecutions—work together for our benefit. In this light, pain is indeed a good thing.

Even if you're not struggling today, you may at some point find yourself on your knees before the throne of grace, alone and in great emotional distress. You want the pain to end *now*. Worldly solutions can only bring temporary relief. You ask God to change your circumstances, fix your situation, and make everything better somehow. But what happens may surprise you. God has a greater purpose in mind than simply changing your circumstances. He wants to deliver you and set you free.

This state of desperation is what drives people to seek counseling. Clients rarely come to me because everything's going fine in their lives. They're in emotional pain, or spiritual distress. The immediate cause might be a troubled relationship, or the loss of a loved one. Symptoms might include depression, anxiety, or some deadly mix of emotions. The pain is real, and must always be taken seriously. But the therapist's challenge is to find the cause.

In cases that involve mental illness or acute trauma like the loss of a loved one, we have to consider the obvious. Even here, it is the *perception* of reality that causes the emotional pain. Moreover, physical symptoms can stem from emotional illness and/or spiritual oppression, and can in turn affect the emotions, exacerbating the pain.

But usually, the source of pain is a set of erroneous beliefs.

So, how then is pain good?

Our pain tells us there is something in us that needs to be healed. *There is something wrong.*

A recent example from my own life illustrates this. I had become accustomed to vigorous physical activity, playing racquetball and swimming on weekends with my daughter. I began to notice an occasional burning in my chest during my racquetball sessions. My doctor said that it was probably acid reflux; nothing to be concerned about. Then I started feeling discomfort while swimming. It would always subside, but as it persisted into the summer, I realized something was wrong. I decided to pay for a full body scan. Again, the test results indicated everything was okay, but the discomfort continued. And, other symptoms appeared. After walking even a few hundred feet, I'd find myself exhausted.

Finally, on the prodding of my wife and friends I went to see a cardiologist. He was very concerned, and sent me for an angiogram. They found that two of my arteries were completely blocked. He was able to clear the arteries, and placed two stints in me, but he confided to my wife Sandra that I had "dodged a bullet."

You see, pain is a good thing. In this case, it told me something was wrong. I thank God that the pain persisted, that I paid attention and found someone who could identify its source. That day, He saved my life.

Emotional pain operates the same way. People seek help from counselors and ministers every day because something is causing pain. Maybe that's why you are reading this book! Something in your life is not working. Some dream or hope you had is dying. God may be allowing circumstances in your life that will lead you into a closer walk with Him, so He can heal you and set you free.

Pain Is a Good Thing!

Most people who seek help simply want someone to stop their pain, not find its underlying cause. It's like going to a medical doctor for back pain; the patient may want a prescription for pain pills. But a good doctor will delve deeper, and recommend physical therapy or other treatment to address the cause.

Most people who seek help simply want someone to stop their pain, not find its underlying cause. It's like going to a medical doctor for back pain: the patient may simply want a prescription for pain pills. But a good doctor will delve deeper, and recommend physical therapy or other treatment to address the cause.

Pain is a gift of God. It tells us we're alive. Yes it hurts, but we know intuitively that it serves a good purpose. If you had accidentally placed your hand over an open flame, wouldn't you want to feel pain? Of course you would. The alternative would be a seriously damaged hand. Certain diseases, such as diabetes and Hansen's disease (leprosy) are particularly insidious because they involve loss of feeling in the extremities. Victims can then suffer wounds that are not detected, often with dire results.

If you can feel pain, then you are alive.

Emotional pain indicates something is wrong.

We instinctively recoil from pain, and avoid it at all costs. Our synapses send messages to the brain which responds by telling the affected area to remove itself from the pain source. If it's possible, we'll immediately flee.

We respond the same way to emotional pain. As Adam and Eve hid because they were naked and ashamed, we try to hide, deny and repress our pain. This allows us to keep the physical feelings associated with stressful emotions at bay. Our brains produce these physical feelings–anxiety, depression, fear, anger—so we'll know that something is wrong.

Since we humans sinned and lost the image of God, we learned to pursue pleasure as an antidote to pain. Our minds created psychological defense mechanisms to deal with the sources of pain, such as denial, repression and anger. We also became adept at creating alternative realities through fantasy. We learned to rationalize, and to neutralize our pain intellectually. We became expert at minimizing and projecting—blaming others for what we were feeling. Some people learned to portray themselves as victims, to avoid acknowledging the cause of the pain in them. In extreme cases, there is dissociation, where the mind actually removes itself from the pain, sometimes splitting into different ego states. These psychological mechanisms share the common purpose of helping us to deny reality. The brain does this to limit the pain.

The point is that without the Truth of God, we all attempt to respond to events in ways that limit our pain and suffering. Pain is "bad," so we want to avoid anything that might cause it, whether it's in a marriage or friendship, at work, or in our beliefs about ourselves. The fallen world is always there to "help" us in this pursuit. But as Christians with the mind of Christ, we can see our emotional pain for what it is: an opportunity to be transformed.

> Pain is an opportunity for transformation!

Since pain simply lets us know something is wrong, we have two choices. The first is to run from pain and avoid it at all costs. The second is to ask God to reveal its source and heal us. Usually, the root of our present pain is some lie we embraced in the past. When we replace that lie with truth, it can no longer cause us emotional pain in the present. Our minds become transformed with the truth, resulting in decreased pain.

Darlene and Ted had been married ten years. Recently, Darlene had become a Christian, but Ted refused to have anything to do with her new faith. Their views of life were now very different. Darlene struggled to find the right way to act toward her husband. She believed in showing him love and respect, but that became difficult when Ted would overspend, drink too much, or watch inappropriate movies. She tried various strategies to cope with her dilemma: going to Bible studies, trying to manipulate Ted into becoming a Christian. Eventually, she simply withdrew her affection. Behind all these things was another emotion: Darlene felt Ted was "controlling" her. Her intense pain finally compelled her to seek counseling.

Pain Is a Good Thing!

As she sat before me, Darlene was feeling deep hatred and entertaining thoughts of divorce. She wanted to save her marriage, but the overriding issue was her feeling of being controlled. It was important that we find the source of that emotion. Rather than avoiding the pain, we walked toward it together. It turned out that Darlene had a perfectionist mother who treated her harshly. She had lived her entire childhood feeling controlled by another person. She learned to believe a lie.

As Darlene brought this trauma before God, He exposed the stronghold that she had erected to protect the lie. Then she heard God tell her the truth: He was in control, not any human being. This truth became personal for her. She was free from the feeling of being controlled by her husband. She could go back to Ted and love him unconditionally—even when he exhibited the same old behavior.

The defense mechanisms we employ to avoid pain are probably necessary to manage our traumatic childhood memories. This is especially true for children who have experienced disaster or abuse. As we get older the traumatic events fade, but the defense mechanisms remain. Now they hurt us more than protect us. To complicate matters, we employ sinful behavior patterns to protect the lies we've embraced. (We discuss this fully in Chapter Seven, Strongholds.) These sinful patterns must be pulled down before we can experience the truth. People who haven't encountered Christ can find some relief by recognizing the information they've been repressing or denying. But until the sinful patterns of resentment, vows, and judgment are torn down, they will remain captive to the beliefs that produced their defense mechanisms. Pain at least forces us to recognize that something bad is there—even if we're not ready to deal with it.

As we experience emotional pain in our day-to-day lives, we're apt to believe that it's rooted in the present. I may feel I'm not a good husband, because my wife has said something critical. I'm in pain, and it's obviously her fault. She made me feel like I'm not up to par, not good enough. My anger focuses on her. But, emotional pain like this is almost always linked to the past—some event where pain was inflicted on us or by us. Emotional pain, like physical pain, tells us something is wrong. It alerts us to something we have believed which is causing our distress—a place in us that needs to experience the truth of Christ. The first thing we must do, then, is ask God to help us.

> Emotional pain indicates that there is a root.

As Jesus pointed out, a bad tree will bear bad fruit and a good tree will bear good fruit. The fruit is simply the visible evidence of what is in that tree. And the tree derives its substance through what is not visible—the root. So, there is an inevitable relationship between the fruit and the root. Pain we experience in the present can be thought of as the fruit, but it points to a root in the past.

Lisa came to me complaining that she felt unloved by her husband Jim. She had a good case; he truly wasn't treating her well. I asked her a simple question: "Did you ever feel unloved before this?" As we began to explore this theme in her life, it became apparent that she had entered the relationship with the belief that she was not loved. It was already living inside her. Her unhappy experience with Jim simply confirmed and validated that belief.

But for Christians, it was never true that we were unloved, or not good enough. As Paul writes, "In love He predestined us to adoption as sons through Jesus Christ to Himself, according to the kind intention of His will ..." (Ephesians 1:4-5). When we truly know that God loves us, we won't experience the feeling of being unloved, even when others mistreat us.

If there is pain, there must be a root preceding the current situation. The importance of pain is it tells us there is something programmed into our minds. Something we believe that is causing pain. God uses the pain for His people to expose the painful source in our life. We then can come to Him with these thoughts and patterns to be transformed by His Word and Truth.

As I work with people who are hurting, God often reveals past traumas and painful events from their lives. They'll sometimes insist that they're "over" it. They've forgiven the offender. They've "let it go." But then, I'll ask the Holy Spirit to reveal any unconfessed sin. That's when God shows them the unforgiveness they're harboring. When it becomes apparent that unreconciled issues remain, I ask another question: "Would you be willing to look at anything the Holy Spirit directs you to?" Sometimes they deny the very existence of the events that are troubling them.

My own life offers a vivid example of this. For many years, I repressed the memory of a childhood molestation. I couldn't see it, and literally did not know it existed. But always, there was pain in my subconscious that found its way out. I had an insistent feeling that something was wrong, that something bad would happen in my future. Even when things went well for me, I would always wait for the other shoe to drop. As I continued to seek God for the root of this pain and belief, I finally saw it.

As we've noted, pain almost always points to underlying resentment, vows, sin, judgment and lies. My emotional pain was like the physical pain caused by my artery condition: a warning light, indicating something was wrong. Without it, I may have never recalled the event that had wrought such damage. If I had ignored it or tried to run away, I would never have been set free. In both situations, God used pain for my good.

It's important that God is the one who reveals these things. That's much better than me as a therapist making an educated guess! In my counseling and praying with people, I try never to go where the Holy Spirit isn't leading. And I never ask them to go where they are not willing. As we allow God to do His gentle work, He reveals the truth, while always protecting His children. We may feel the pain, sometimes intensely. But rarely will the process overwhelm us. God is a good and gracious healer.

> God uses pain for our good.

Not only does emotional pain act as a catalyst by indicating that something is wrong; it is also the very thing God uses to reveal what's in our hearts. God has promised us that He will keep us from harm and complete the work that He began in us. He allows hardship into our lives to test us, prove us, prune us, and chasten our flesh.

"My son, despise not thou the chastening of the Lord, nor faint when thou art rebuked of him; For whom the Lord loveth he chasteneth, and scourgeth every son

whom he receiveth. If ye endure chastening, God dealeth with you as with sons; for what son is he whom the father chasteneth not? But if ye be without chastisement, whereof all are partakers, then are ye bastards, and not sons. Furthermore we have had fathers of our flesh which corrected us, and we gave them reverence: shall we not much rather be in subjection unto the Father of spirits, and live? For they verily for a few days chastened us after their own pleasure; but he for our profit, that we might be partakers of his holiness. Now no chastening for the present seemeth to be joyous, but grievous: nevertheless afterward it yieldeth the peaceable fruit of righteousness unto them which are exercised thereby" (Hebrews 12:5-11).

As we've noted, the word *"chasten"* really means *hardship*. Yes, God disciplines those He loves. In this scripture, it is clear that God chastens *all* His children—not just rebellious or disobedient ones. God chastens us for our profit, in order to work His holiness in us. Just as Christ obeyed His Father, He wants us to obey (*listen attentively*) during life's hardships.

Pain points to what is in us. In hard times, it's important to pay attention to what our thoughts are telling us, and the words that come out of our mouths. Hardship triggers the expression of strongholds through sin, pain, and what we believe. This is how suffering chastens us—by revealing these things. If we love God, we respond by listening, and speaking with Him, putting away our self-reliance. He is present, as the scripture says: "We have this treasure in earthen vessels, that the surpassing greatness of the power may be of God, and not from ourselves" (1 Corinthians 4:7).

Hard times make us depend on God. We recognize that only Christ can deliver us. We see the sin we have tolerated, and emerge at last from our denial, repression, dissociation, minimization, and blaming. We bring these false beliefs to him to exchange for the truth. We stop living according to our old nature, deceived and enslaved to sin. We begin living according to our new identity in Christ, holy and righteous.

We experience Christ in our Pain.

Through pain, we have the privilege of sharing the sufferings of Jesus. This is an important truth that many people miss. Christians elevate suffering as a noble thing when it's associated with official ministry-related activities. We envision suffering for Christ as an exotic experience on some faraway mission field. But the suffering that Jesus experienced was real, intimate and personal.

He was misunderstood—even by His closest friends. His own family renounced Him. The people he had walked with for years abandoned Him when the chips were down. One of them sold him out, for money! Then, he endured cruel beatings and a phony trial. He was framed, falsely convicted, and sent to a horrific execution. On the way, people who had been his allies openly mocked him. The nation that should have welcomed Him as king treated Him like scum.

I have never known that kind of suffering. How can I truly fellowship with the sufferings of Christ? Yet, the Apostle Paul states that "we complete the afflictions of Christ," and Jesus exhorted us to pick up our cross daily. Jesus bore the penalty for my sin—the pain I should have experienced. Now, I'm no longer under condemnation. When I continue to experience pain because of my lingering sin, Jesus is there, bearing it with me. My suffering is now His suffering.

On the other hand, if I run from my pain, I'm not accepting what is real in my flesh. And if I reject reality, how can I connect with Jesus in that pain? God only lives in reality. When I run from pain, I'm running from Him. When I turn and go towards my fears, lies, and pain, I find Jesus. That is where He is—in my pain! There, He provides strength, comfort, and safety. This then is where I join with him, and the Greek word translated "join" in the scriptures also means *peace*. In my pain is where I find peace, joining with Him in my suffering, which He made His own. Peace is not placidity, or the absence of pain. Peace is what we find in the garden with Christ, knowing even through our travails that God is working His will in us.

So, there are several aspects to the suffering God brings to us: We complete the afflictions of Christ. We pick up and carry our cross daily. We fellowship with the sufferings of Christ. We allow the Holy Spirit in us to crucify the flesh, just as Christ allowed His flesh to be crucified for us. We trust Him in our pain, rather than denying Him in our pain.

This has real-life applications. When Joe discovered that his wife Annie was having an affair with a coworker, he was understandably distraught.

He had tried for years to please her, but felt like a failure. This bred a deep anger in him, which Annie tried several times to address. He interpreted her words as a condemnation; he just wasn't good enough for her. This continued for years. He refused to address his pain and the sense of "not being good enough." Even though it was this deep sense of inadequacy that kept him angry and resistant to his wife's attempts to better their relationship, he blamed *her* for his feelings. Finally she went to another man, just to be heard. Her husband wasn't listening.

Both Joe and Annie were running ran from their pain: He ran to anger, she eventually ran to sin. They both were holding deep resentment in their hearts: Joe had never believed he was good enough, and she never believed that people cared about what she had to say. So here they met. His lies were perpetuated by her actions—and hers by his. They both used unregenerate means to deal with the problem. When the pain became too great, they both withdrew their hearts, and eventually themselves from the relationship.

If Joe and Annie had seen their pain as a warning of something wrong, and been willing to confront themselves rather than each other, they could have restored their marriage. Instead, they chose other methods to deal with their emotions.

"I could never forgive her!" Joe told me in a moment of raw anger. The pain was simply too great. I explained that he was not alone in his pain; Jesus was there with him. And there is no limit to God's forgiveness.

Meanwhile, Annie repented. Now it was up to Joe to realize that by walking toward his pain, he would join Jesus. The Lord had already taken it, and was there to offer His support and comfort. Thankfully, Joe followed the Lord's direction and forgave Annie. He was then able to move forward and receive his own healing.

Annie had a more difficult time forgiving Joe. They continued to struggle, as she blamed him for her sin. Her guilt made it hard for her to face her actions. Instead of bringing this to Christ, she continued to blame Joe. Eventually, Annie realized that Jesus had always been present in her life— even when she was sinning. He was there, taking her sin. That's how much

He loved her! When she walked into the pain of her own sin, she found Jesus there—along with forgiveness and cleansing.

Annie and Joe continue to deal with the hurts of their past. But by refusing to retreat from their pain, they now know the peace that comes from joining Christ in the midst of it.

I often ask people to acknowledge God in the midst of their pain. This seems strange, but is really very helpful. We simply ask God to show us where the pain is coming from, in the belief that it's there to reveal something we need to see. I must find the plank in my own eye before blaming others. I must not run from my pain. By asking God, I allow Him to reveal its source—the lies I have believed.

CHAPTER SIX

Lies We Believe: Our False Reality

They exchanged the truth of God for a lie. (ROMANS 1:25)

Scripture tells us that to be transformed, we must have our minds renewed (Romans 12:1-2). But renewed from what? As the Bible also says, our minds have been *deceived*. So to experience true change, we must be cleansed of the lies we have embraced.

Our beliefs and sense of reality are all based on our *experiences*. They shape the way we perceive ourselves, others, and yes, even God. As we all know, many of these experiences are negative, and have led us to believe things that aren't true. These lies, formed during specific life events, become our reality. They're reinforced over time through similar subsequent events. And they cause us emotional pain. Most people resort to sin to take this pain away, including Christians. So what is the way out? We begin with the first step: identifying the lies that have lodged in our minds, so that the truth of Christ can renew us.

Imagine for a moment that your mind is a computer. Like any computer, it runs on a program. Sounds simple enough, right? But here's the important part: The program currently running in your mind is based on your life experiences—what you learned as a child. Even more, it is based on the sin you were born into. So, it's a flawed program! It has glitches that cause you to malfunction, similar to a computer virus. These glitches are our false beliefs.

We'll refer to this computer program as our *false reality*. It's not the truth, but it is all we know, and thus becomes truth to *us*. We can't grasp anything outside of it. This is why it is so important to identify our lies, because they contradict the truth in Christ. Our false reality is not God's reality. We need to be transformed.

Once we accept our need for transformation, we may attempt to override our false beliefs with something other than God's truth. But we can't simply combat lies with new information. We must replace them with something more powerful—the truth, through Christ. He *is* the Truth (John 14:6).

In the following pages we'll identify some common lies. Then, we'll explain how they affect us, how we use sinful behavior to alleviate our pain, and most importantly, how we can experience the transforming power of Christ. We'll learn to speak His truth into our minds, replacing our false reality.

In His finished work on the cross, Jesus destroyed our need to rely on our own efforts—our own *works*. How does this relate to the dysfunction in our lives? When we recognize the lies we have believed—and each lie is associated with pain and sin—then we realize that we've spent our lives *working* to alleviate the pain those lies have caused. Change comes when we walk *into* our pain with Christ, and allow Him to replace each lie with the truth. No longer do we have to work to alleviate the pain, or use sin and temporary pleasure to take it away. We are transformed.

Below are some of the false beliefs I've heard people express. See how many of them are familiar to you:

Lies We Believe

- I'm not good enough.
- People don't listen to me.
- People don't care.
- People can't be trusted.
- People don't trust *me*.
- People always lie.
- I'm not loved.
- I'm unwanted.
- I'm dirty.
- People always leave me.
- I'm alone.
- I'm abandoned.
- I don't like myself.
- I hate myself.
- I can't do anything right.
- I'm misunderstood.
- I'm weak.
- I'm unstable.
- I'm overwhelmed.
- I'm inadequate.
- I'm stupid.
- I'm afraid.
- I'm disapproved.
- I'm doomed.
- I'm going to be destroyed.
- People won't help me.
- I'm different.
- I'm not a real man.
- I'm not a real woman.
- I'll never change.
- I'm terrified.
- There's always a catch.

- I'm not important.
- I'm not smart enough.
- I'm not connected.
- I can't do it.
- I'm a loser.
- I'm a failure.
- I'm going to fail.
- My life is over.
- I'm not a good wife.
- I'm not a good husband.
- People don't like me.
- I don't fit in.
- I'm different.
- I don't have enough.
- My needs won't be met.
- Everything is my fault.
- Bad things will happen.
- Things will never change.
- People provoke me.
- People hate me.
- People take advantage of me.
- I'm not whole.
- I'm not normal.
- I'm not OK.
- I'm incomplete.
- I'm invisible.
- Nobody notices me.
- I'm not needed.
- I'm betrayed.
- I'm not worthy.
- People think I'm crazy.

- I'm out of control.
- I can't rest.
- Life is too difficult.
- I'm trapped.
- I must make it on my own.
- I'm not safe.
- I'm empty.
- People don't believe me.
- I'm ugly.
- I'm used.
- I'm not a good provider.
- I can't make decisions.
- I'm unappreciated.
- I'm on my own.
- People break their promises.
- I'm helpless.
- I'm hopeless.
- Things won't get better.
- I'm deceived.
- Something's wrong with me.
- I won't amount to anything.
- I don't exist.
- I don't matter.
- I'm being controlled.
- I'm guilty.
- I'm seduced.
- I'm rejected.
- I'm evil.
- I'm wrong.
- I'm going to fail.

Often when I counsel clients, I'll present them with this list of lies, and ask them to check off the ones that pertain to them, grading their relative strength from one to ten. If the belief is very strong and always present, it's a ten—and so on. Each of these lies may contain an element of truth. For example, if I attempted to perform brain surgery, I certainly wouldn't be *good enough*! What makes them lies is not their relationship to objective facts, but the hold they exert on us, regardless of the facts. These false beliefs reside deep in the soul of a person. They seize our minds and hearts, causing us pain. If we're honest, we'll acknowledge that several of them exist in our lives to one degree or another.

Now, if these beliefs reflect what we truly feel, how can they be false? They may even be borne out in our everyday experience. But in Christ — in our renewed spiritual selves — none of these things is true. That is why they are lies. Accepting lies has been part of the human condition from the beginning. We see this in the opening chapters of Genesis, when the serpent convinced Eve that she was missing something. To find true fulfillment, she would need to eat that fruit. Then, Eve would be like God. But she and Adam *already* bore the image of God! It was all a lie—like the lies we believe about ourselves. We are renewed in Christ, with God's image restored, but we tend to believe we're still missing something.

DON'T BELIEVE WHAT YOU BELIEVE!

It's hard to accept responsibility for the things we believe. We tend to blame them on events and circumstances in our lives. If I believe that I am unloved, I'll find confirmation in everyday events.

You'll remember Ted from the previous chapter. During counseling, he divulged to me that when his wife failed to make him breakfast, he took it as proof that she didn't love him. Like all of us, he attributed his beliefs to objective events. But it's never the event that causes our pain; it's *what we believe about the event.*

Many of us believe we are unloved, as Ted did. We can try to change our feelings by getting someone to love us, or loving ourselves, or telling ourselves that we're loved. We may practice verbal self-affirmation, or in the case of Christians, quote scripture to ourselves. But notice, the focus is always on *self*. And that is part of the deception!

Another person in Ted's situation might have dismissed the experience as insignificant. But as Ted's computer brain processed the data, its faulty programming led to a bad conclusion. The lie he had come to believe defiled the truth. And as long as that lie remains, the conclusion will always be the same.

So how do we stop believing what we believe? To recall the words of Jesus, "With men it is impossible, but with God all things are possible." We may be able to recognize the irrationality of our beliefs, but apart from the truth of God, they will continue to contaminate our thinking and emotions. We cannot change ourselves through effort or intellectual insight. The problem is in our programming. This becomes most evident when we experience crisis. Stressful experiences trigger our false beliefs, without fail. Our code must be rewritten! The original code was written by the deceiver of our souls. The new one can only be written by the One who overcame the deceiver—Christ, who is living in us.

So, how do we uncover the lies that are in us? After all, if we're truly deceived, that means we *can't see* the truth.

How do we stop blaming events and others for our pain, and start recognizing the beliefs that are really causing it?

EXPOSING OUR HEARTS

Jesus and Paul give us two very efficient ways of uncovering the lies in us. In the Old Testament, Jeremiah declares, "The heart is more deceitful than all else and is desperately sick. Who can understand it?" He answers that question in the next verse: "I the Lord search the heart, I test the mind, even to give to each man according to his ways." (Jeremiah 17: 9-10). As we've noted, Jesus Christ delivered a great insight about human nature when he exhorted us to remove the planks in our own eyes—and then we'd see clearly to help our brother with the speck in his. But how do we find those planks in our eyes? A few verses later, Jesus gives us a clue: "Ask and it shall be given to you; seek, and you shall find; knock, and it shall be opened to you." (Matthew 7:7). If we ask Him, He'll show us.

What are these planks, anyway? Surely not good things, if they prevent us from seeing what's happening around us! The word translated *plank* could refer to a beam in a house, or a pillar that holds up a building. We might think of the planks in our lives as those beliefs that hold up our ways of thinking. We must locate them, and remove them with God's truth. If we ask, we will receive. *But, we must ask.*

Then, *we must listen.* One of the ways we can discover our false beliefs is by listening to what comes out of our own mouths. Jesus also put his finger on this: "The good man out of the good treasure of his heart brings forth what is good; and the evil man out of the evil treasure brings forth what is evil; for his mouth speaks from that which fills his heart." (Luke 6:45). By paying attention to our words, we'll learn what's really in our hearts: the lies as well as truth, and the issues that trouble us.

This is very difficult to do. When we're confronted with what we've actually said, we're often tempted to deny it. Sometimes in counseling I'll repeat what people say, and the response is, "Well, that's not what I meant!"

It's hard to face our own words, because that would mean confronting the lies in our hearts. We have many ways of escaping from pain. Refusing to listen to our own words is one of them.

This is why it's so important to enlist the help of others. A skilled counselor can help us hear the things we don't want to. The scriptures repeatedly tell us to seek counsel: "By the mouth of two or three witnesses every fact shall be confirmed." (Deuteronomy 19:15, Matthew 18:16). This is God's gift to us. We need others to listen and give us feedback, not necessarily to interpret what we mean, but simply to reflect back what we've said. That's how the issues of the heart emerge. When Ted told me that his wife didn't love him, his words betrayed the issue of his heart. He believed that he was unloved. This was much deeper than a one-time event. It was a long-standing, chronic belief that had been programmed into his brain.

When clients bring up incidents like this, I usually ask them if they ever felt this feeling prior to the recent event. They almost always say yes. This helps them realize that the person they're blaming is not the cause, but the current trigger of that belief.

Most people are very willing to tell the stories of their lives: the divorce, betrayal and abuse; the times they were hurt by others. What they rarely do is pay attention to the beliefs those stories reveal. Telling the story does not change the story, any more than it can the erase the lie and remove the pain. At best, it can *reveal* the lie behind the experience — if we're looking for it.

TAKING OUR THOUGHTS CAPTIVE

In a verse we quote often, Paul states that "The weapons of our warfare are not of the flesh, but divinely powerful for the destruction of fortresses." He goes on to model what we should be doing: "We are destroying speculations and every lofty thing raised up against the knowledge of God, and we are taking every thought captive to the obedience of Christ ..." (2 Corinthians 10: 4-5) Taking our thoughts captive is foreign to us because we're more accustomed to simply denying them. Our negative beliefs cause us pain, so we immediately try to push them away. We may even ask God to remove them. But He doesn't. To take our thoughts captive, we must admit that they are in us. We must accept these thoughts as real, not try to rationalize them or push them away. Many of us have been taught to *think positive*. But this is not what the scripture directs us to do. Denying our negative thoughts is the self's way of dealing with them.

But let's consider what "taking our thoughts captive to the obedience of Christ" might mean. The word "obedience" means to *listen attentively*. We are to take our every thought to Jesus, and then listen as he tells us the truth—and what we are to do. This process—capturing our thoughts, and listening—is an important part of our spiritual warfare.

All of us have acquired the habit of listening, but it's not usually to God. Unfortunately, even Christians listen to the voices of this world. We attempt to get rid of lies through positive thinking. Not believing that God in us is the source of all truth, we seek natural solutions for our problems. But Christ does live in us, and we can, as Paul said, "put on the mind of Christ." What is the mind of Christ? Is it not Jesus living in us through the Holy Spirit? As Christians, we need not avoid our negative thoughts and words as sin, because there is no longer any condemnation for sin. We can simply accept them as God's way of revealing our hearts to us. He is dedicated to healing us daily, so when we ask, He reveals. He gives us the ability to catch our thoughts, words and lies, and convinces us of their destructive nature. When we agree with Him (confess), He sets us free.

THE BODY OF CHRIST

The fourth way that we are exposed is through the fellowship of our brothers and sisters in Christ. We're commanded to go to those who have offended us, and to those we have offended. This is one of God's primary ways of revealing our sin and deception. As we trust our brothers and sisters, and learn to hear Christ in them, we receive truth about ourselves. Jesus said, "For where two or three have gathered together in my name, there I am in their midst." (Matthew 1:20). And James tells us, "He who turns a sinner from the error of his way will save his soul from death, and will cover a multitude of sins." (James 5:20). Interaction with fellow Christians is very important in revealing our lies and sin.

For this all to work, we must see how essential the Body of Christ is for our spiritual survival. As Paul said, "...If one member suffers, all the members suffer with it; if one member is honored, all the members rejoice with it" (1 Corinthians 12:26) The church must foster personal relationships in such a way that people realize they can't exist without each other. That means giving up the individualistic spirit that is so prevalent in our age. It also means giving up our natural tendency to judge others. Each regenerated man, woman and child is manifesting Christ in a unique way. If we're wise we'll learn to recognize that, instead of judging our fellow-believers, condemning them for their sin, and imposing unnecessary rules on them.

An important part of our healing is confession. This involves risk, as we expose our pain and sin to each other. It means learning to depend on each other; living life together. We must allow others to speak into our lives, and they must do the same. No amount of programs can accomplish this in us. This is the inheritance of everyone who has been regenerated by the Spirit of God and bears God's image. As Paul exhorted the Ephesians, "... Speaking the truth in love, we are to grow up in all aspects into Him, who is the head, even Christ, from whom the whole body, being fitted and held together by that which every joint supplies, according to the proper working of each individual part, causes the growth of the body for the building up of itself in love" (Ephesians 4:15-16). This is the kind of love that puts the interests of others first, that Jesus alluded to when he said, "I and the Father are one."

He pointed the way for us as His life was about to end: "By this all men will know that you are My disciples, if you have love for one another" (John 13:35). And as John later noted, "...The one who does not love his brother whom he has seen, cannot love God whom he has not seen" (1 John 4:20).

This kind of interdependence is largely missing in the Church today. Something must take place in our relationships. But as long as we cling to the lies sown in us through sin, our relationships will be superficial at best.

THE FATHER OF LIES

"You are of your father the devil, and you want to do the desires of your father. He was a murderer from the beginning, and does not stand in the truth because there is no truth in him. Whenever he speaks a lie, he speaks from his own nature, for he is a liar and the father of lies" (John 8:44).

Satan is our adversary. As the books of Job and Revelation make clear, he is our accuser before God — a relentless prosecutor who does not have our good in mind. We must realize that when we approach God on the basis of our own goodness, our adversary will always have legal grounds against us. As the scripture says, "For all of us have become like one who is unclean, and all our righteous deeds are like a filthy garment" (Isaiah 64:6).

When Jesus said, "Agree with your adversary quickly," He was not intimating that we should compromise with the devil. Rather, when Satan accuses us of some sin or flaw, it is to our advantage to agree quickly and acknowledge our shortcomings. The key is not to argue with the devil about our own righteousness. This is in essence what we do when we try to solve our sin and deception problems with our own wisdom and intellect. Then, the adversary will always have legal grounds to "cast [us] into prison" as Jesus warned.

Waging War

"Be of sober spirit, be on the alert. Your adversary, the devil, prowls about like a roaring lion, seeking someone to devour" (1 Peter 5:8).

What gives Satan the right to seize upon God's children and devour them? Didn't Jesus say of us, "No one shall snatch them out of my hand"? (John 10:28). He also said, "I guarded them, and not one of them perished but the son of perdition..." (John 17:12).

Then, does Satan have access to us? Demons can and do harass God's children through their untransformed minds. It is important to realize that deception is Satan's chief method of attack. As long as we remain deceived in our minds, the enemy can oppress us. It is in those areas of deception that the forces of darkness gain entrance.

The word entice, which we see in scripture, means to deceive. Jesus spoke of events that would deceive even God's elect, if it were possible. This is why Paul exhorts us to "...Take up the full armor of God, that you may be able to resist in the evil day, and having done everything, to stand firm" (Ephesians 6:13). He goes on to describe "the shield of faith, with which you will be able to extinguish all the flaming missiles of the evil one. And take the helmet of salvation and the sword of the Sprit which is the word of God" (Ephesians 6:16-17).

Those fiery missiles of the evil one can only penetrate where lies exist. Does a part of me feel unloved? That's where Satan can accuse me. In that corner of my soul, I doubt the very word of God. In the areas where I know and accept the truth, I cannot be accused. When Jesus was tempted in the desert, he stood against Satan's powerful assault and did not succumb to the lie. We can do the same. But in our case, the lie is already in us, from birth. As David lamented, "Behold, I was brought forth in iniquity, and in sin my mother conceived me (Psalm 51:5 Our situation is desperate, but God has not left us defenseless. Jesus is more than our example; He's our defender and advocate.

When Satan decided to tempt Job, he found a vulnerable spot in Job's fear. Job had a beautiful family and a nice life. No doubt, he feared losing all that. In the midst of his trials, Job said, "For what I fear comes upon me, and what I dread befalls me" (Job 3:25). But as we learn from the rest of Job's story, God is greater than the enemy. And even if the lies in our hearts accuse us, as John said, "God is greater than our hearts, and knows all things" (1 John 3:20).

As we are transformed, the enemy loses his power to deceive us. He cannot affect us where his lies are rooted out. He is only a roaring lion, now — but the roars are silenced by the blood of the Lamb. Our warfare is in the spiritual realm, and now that we have received the Spirit of God, the battle is waged predominantly in our minds. Eve was deceived — convinced of something false in her mind — and then she transgressed. If the enemy is harassing and scaring you, it's all deception. It's him strutting about like a roaring lion. But in the presence of Christ, this lion has no power.

As we all know, our flesh is weak and we're vulnerable to fear. This is a result of chemical reactions in our bodies. By placing our hope in the God who is truth and perfect love, we can cast out fear. Our real task is to believe in Him. God is always working to reveal the deception in our minds and hearts. As he does, the enemy loses ground against our flesh. He has no access to our spirits, since the image of God has been restored in us. We must recognize that as higher beings indwelt by the Spirit of God, the demonic realms have no real power. All they can do is trick us.
I often hear Christians say, "Satan is putting thoughts in my mind!" They attribute their negative or sinful thoughts to the enemy. I have a very different view. I believe these thoughts and beliefs are already programmed into our minds, causing us to act in sinful ways. Sin is deceptive. Deception implies that there is something we cannot see. Why would the enemy

want us to see our negative beliefs and sinful thoughts? His real ploy is to convince us his program of self-help will work in conquering sin!

I would submit that when we find these things in our hearts and minds, it is actually God revealing them to us. How else could we see them as areas in need of change? Only God in us is able to reveal the truth to us.

Trina was a teenage client who had a wonderful revelation of God's love during a counseling session. She felt Him telling her personally how much He loved her. But as soon she left our session, she felt a powerful urge to have sex with her boyfriend. She was confused. "How could that be God?" she asked, quite reasonably.

"Do you belong to God?" I asked her.
"Yes."
"Didn't we ask Him to show us the truth?"
"Well, yes."

"OK. He's simply showing you what's in your mind and heart. He's pointing out your sin to you."

Trina confessed the sin in her mind. That was the first step toward victory. When sin and lies are revealed to us, they're exposed to the light. That's a good thing. But most of us aren't taught what to do with these things, so we're disturbed when they come to our attention. We re told they are sinful, so we must work to get rid of them. But Scripture tells us to take them captive to Jesus, confess them and have them cleansed. This is Spiritual warfare at its best.

God is forever faithful to His children, working in us to reveal our lies and sin. It is these that cause the emotional pain we struggle with. Transformation is about change in our flesh and carnal minds—our natural selves. It is never about who we really are in Christ. Our deception constitutes the very heart of the strongholds that must be torn down for our transformation to begin.

CHAPTER SEVEN

Strongholds

For though we walk in the flesh, we do not war according to the flesh, for the weapons of our warfare are not of the flesh, but divinely powerful for the destruction of fortresses. We are destroying speculations and every lofty thing raised up against the knowledge of God, and we are taking every thought captive to the obedience of Christ.

(2 CORINTHIANS 10:3-5)

What is a *stronghold*? The word has become popular in Christian circles even though it only occurs once in scripture. (It's translated *fortresses* in the above passage.) There is much debate over whether a Christian, born again of the Spirit of God, can have an area where God's truth does not reach. And of course, Christians disagree over the degree of influence demonic spirits can have in a believer's life.

Let's use a simple image to convey what we mean by a stronghold. Imagine a medieval city with thick, high stone walls. In earlier times, cities were built as fortresses to protect from invaders. The walls protected the inhabitants inside, and prevented outsiders from coming in. They were designed to be intimidating and absolutely secure. The higher and thicker, the better. Now, imagine that such a fortress exists in your own mind. This is what we're dealing with.

Our task is to identify the strongholds in our lives, and tear them down. Before we can do that we must understand them. What are they made of? Certainly, they're evil, or Paul wouldn't be telling us to cast them down. He makes it clear that we're dealing in the realm of the mind—our thoughts. In other passages, he describes how we can be deceived in our minds. The passage above mentions *speculations*, which could also be called *imaginations* or *reasonings*—the stuff of our thoughts and beliefs. These are the arguments, ideologies, philosophies, and rationales that we use to support the strongholds in our lives. In another translation they're described as *vain*—useless and empty. They are diametrically opposed to the knowledge of Christ. How do we know this? Because we're told to tear them down. And we're further told to be transformed by the *renewing* of our minds.

The fact is, all people have these internal strongholds—even Christians. They're
designed to protect us, and offer a sense of security. This is important to grasp.
Like medieval townsfolk, we erect walls because we think we won't survive without them. This is why we cling to them and protect them fiercely. But as
Christians we have no more need of such false protection. God is transforming us,
conforming us to the image of His son. So, these internal fortresses serve no beneficial
function in our lives. In fact, they hinder our spiritual well-being.

We must destroy these strongholds using the instructions of scripture. There is no other way to combat them. We cannot move, shake, break, battle or tear them down through our own efforts. We cannot negotiate with them, persuade them or talk them into going away. They are very resilient. They cannot be forced, reasoned or regulated away, and they don't go away with time. They are spiritually powerful, so they don't self-destruct or wither away.

It is equally futile to ask people to come out of their strongholds, or destroy them. They can't. Strongholds can only be overcome through the power of Christ Himself. We must use the weapons He gives us, and yield ourselves as instruments of righteousness, as Paul describes in Romans 6:12-14. And we must pick up the *weapons* of righteousness God provides us. What are these weapons, and how do we use them? That is what we'll explore in this chapter.

We'll start by explaining what makes up a stronghold and how it forms in our minds. It usually begins when we're young—even in the womb. We're all descendants of fallen people, and the sins of our ancestors can influence our own lives. Whatever the cause, walls of protection are erected in our minds, like the fortresses we pictured earlier. Over time, the walls get thicker and higher, becoming impregnable. They can only be torn down with spiritual weapons. This is an important task, and not for the faint of heart. The first step is to identify the strongholds that are in us.

IDENTIFYING STRONGHOLDS

Do you feel trapped, like you're in a prison? This is evidence of a stronghold in your life. Paradoxically, the stronghold can also make you feel safe, protected from others and the world. The same fortress that offers you protection holds you captive. You can't escape through will-power or self-effort. Only the blood of Christ can bring your freedom.

And you will only accomplish it by waging war with spiritual weapons.

> A stronghold is like a fortress that provides a false sense of protection and security.

Mary was a young woman who suffered deep emotional pain for years. As a girl, she was physically beaten by her father and neglected by her mother. Through each painful episode, she learned to protect herself with the only tools she had available: making vows, pronouncing judgment, and holding unforgiveness (resentment) in her heart.

No one was there to teach Mary the ways of God: how much He loved her, how He viewed her, how she could receive His forgiveness and forgive others. Instead, she was left to suffer under the deception of sin—that which she was born into, and that which others perpetrated against her. The enemy of her soul gained a powerful foothold in her young life, and over time each lie became a stronghold. Mary wasn't aware of them, but could feel their effect. She would speak of feeling "trapped", "unloved"," unworthy", or "always wrong." The list was long.

Mary tried desperately to deal with her pain through a range of futile behaviors. She clung to her vows, judgment and unforgiveness. She separated herself from others. She indulged in sexual sin in a futile effort to feel good about herself. She worked hard at her career to prove her worth. She tried to "be good."

The walls just got thicker and higher.

Now as an adult, Mary finds herself disconnected from others, afraid to open her heart to anyone. When she sought approval as a child, her parents responded with more neglect and abuse. Nothing she did was good enough. As a result, she now strives constantly to make others happy, whatever the cost. Her quest for love led her only to sin and more pain.

Mary's dysfunctional behavior was a sure sign that she harbored deception and strongholds in her life. And it showed in the confessions of her heart. She wants to be able to open her heart to others without fear of being hurt. She is trusting God to lead her into the freedom she has always longed for.

WEAPONS OF RIGHTEOUSNESS

Whether the fortress walls are ten feet high or a thousand, only spiritual weapons are powerful enough to tear them down. We have a picture of this in the biblical story of the battle of Jericho (Joshua 6, Hebrews 11:30-31). The Israelites' strategy was to march around the city, then blow their trumpets and shout—not an impressive plan from a human perspective. That was the point—they couldn't rely on their human ability. They needed to follow God's instructions, but the battle was His.

ANATOMY OF A STRONGHOLD

What comprises a stronghold? And what makes it *strong*? As Mary's story illustrates, these fortresses can exert a powerful hold on us. They're hard to penetrate and difficult to breach, like the walls of Jericho. Many in the Christian community view them as demonic fortresses, and attack them by praying against Satan and his hosts. But the apostle Paul speaks of imaginations and thoughts—things that exist in our own minds and hearts. It is in our minds that we are deceived. Certainly, when we harbor entrenched sin demons can oppress us, but even then God has great news: Jesus destroyed the works of Satan, making a spectacle of principalities and the powers of darkness. Satan is the most cunning of creatures, as deceptive in our lives as he was in the Garden of Eden. But in Christ Jesus, we have weapons of righteousness to destroy his work.

> The lie (deception) is the main component of the stronghold.

At the center of every stronghold is a lie. This is the main component—the king of the fortress, as it were. It's something we believe which brings us emotional pain (as we discussed in Chapter 6, *The Lies We Believe*). It usually comes into our minds through an event (e.g., abuse, neglect, etc.) by which we're deceived us into believing something that is not true. We then erect structures to protect ourselves—to prevent us from feeling the pain of the lie.

Mary believed she was unloved. The emotional pain from that lie was so overwhelming that she was compelled to protect herself from further damage. The methods she used might be called weapons of unrighteousness: sin, resentment, judgment, and vows. They formed an impenetrable barrier to keep her from feeling the pain of the lie. She had also embraced other lies, each producing its own pain. And each one was protected by more sin, vows, resentment and judgment. But Mary can learn to use God's weapons of righteousness, and like the Israelites at Jericho, watch the walls come tumbling down.

Like Mary, most of us were never taught how to forgive as children. There was no one to speak the truth to us in our hurtful experiences. We've all had thoughts like *nobody loves me,* or *nobody wants me*. Had we been taught God's way, we could have taken those thoughts captive to Christ, and allowed Him to speak truth into our hearts. Instead, like Mary, we use sin, resentment/unforgiveness, judgment, and vows to manage our pain. These four components, which we'll call the *defensive four*, comprise a stronghold in us, which protects us from feeling the emotional pain from the lies we believe. The stronghold acts to hold the lie in place, and its effect is to torment and defile us. To receive the truth of Christ in those areas of deception, we must tear down the strongholds using weapons of righteousness. But first, we must understand the false weapons we've been using—and why they don't work.

THE FALSE PROTECTORS

1. Sin
Sin is a critical part of a stronghold. We use it to protect ourselves from our emotional pain. But of course, its pleasure is only temporary. Like drug addicts, we require more and more of it to feel good. We become adept at finding new and different ways to sin. And we become expert at making excuses and covering up our guilt. Thus, sin always leads to more problems. As scripture says, the inevitable consequence of sin is more sin (1 Timothy 4:2, Titus 1:15). We become trapped in it, committing more sin in greater variety.

The Bible describes men who are *given over* to their sin. We lose control of our sin, and instead it controls us—like any addiction. To think we can control sin is a delusion in the first place. Sin leads to destruction; there is no other outcome. In fact, the scripture says *whatever* does not spring from faith in Christ is sin (Hebrews 3:12; 4:6; 4:11; Romans 11:20-21). This is why we can never find healing or salvation simply by being moral. Sin holds us captive and it is a cruel master. Paul conveyed the agonizing struggle that sin causes with these familiar words: "…The good that I wish, I do not do; but I practice the very evil that I do not wish" (Romans 7:14-25).

As we all know, sin takes many forms: jealousy, greed, anger, violence, substance abuse, lust, adultery, lying, stealing. But those are only the more blatant ones. What about blaming, slandering others, or withdrawing love? These qualify too. They all serve the purpose of helping us deal with the pain of deception in our flesh. So in a perverse way, sin becomes our protector. It works to keep us from seeing the lies in us and feeling the pain. But of course, sin eventually brings its own pain. As God warned Cain at the beginning of mankind's descent into depravity, sin "crouches at the door." It's always waiting, ready to be ignited at any moment of temptation.

The fall of man brought with it a depth of corruption far more devastating than we can imagine. Until we're regenerated by the new birth, we're helpless to fight it. Even as believers, as Paul laments and all of us have experienced, sin continues to manifest in our flesh. Yet as Paul wrote, we are no longer of the flesh, but of the spirit. This is the good news of the gospel. Nothing can separate us from God's love. We grapple with sin, but this is no longer who we are. So why do we still struggle? To prove that it is God's power working in us—not our own. God is using all these things—even our sin—for our benefit.

Sin and deception must be dealt with on a daily basis. They are continually being forgiven by the blood of Christ, but we reap their effects until we confess and allow God to cleanse us. The poison of sin infiltrates every part of our old nature. As the scripture tells us, the new nature wars against the old. We must confess all sin from the past to remove its evil consequences. This is a daunting task, but we depend on God to show us the places He wants to transform. Paradoxically, we cannot be free until we know that we are *already* free. We are dead to sin, and now must conquer the areas of our minds that don't know that.

2. Resentment and Unforgiveness

Another self-protection mechanism is allowing resentment and unforgiveness to take root in our hearts. When someone offends us, we retreat into resentment, hardening our hearts to avoid feeling the pain the incident has caused. This goes hand in hand with unforgiveness. This is the second integral component of a stronghold. Together with sin, judgment and vows, it works powerfully to keep us trapped.

3. Judgment

Jesus warned us about this common human tendency: "Do not judge, lest you be judged yourselves" (Matthew 7:1). We draw unfair conclusions about other people—who or what they are—based on false information, or our own bitterness. Our minds use this to prevent us from seeing our own deception. We accuse others to avoid the pain of what we really believe about ourselves. If Todd says to his wife, "You make me feel stupid," it's a good indicator that this belief is already lodged in his mind. He may even take it a step further, and tell her, "*You're* stupid!" Instead of facing his false belief, which would be unbearably painful, he points the finger outward. Psychologists refer to this as projection or transference. *Judgment* thus forms another part of the stronghold, further trapping and imprisoning us.

4) Vows

Jesus addressed our tendency to make *false vows*, saying, "But I say to you, make no oath at all ...But let your statement be, 'Yes, yes' or 'No, no;' and anything beyond these is of evil" (Matthew 5:34,37).

What are vows? A vow is simply a promise we make to others or ourselves. Most of us are familiar with the marriage vow, wherein we promise to love, honor and obey another person. But the vows we're concerned with here are destructive, made out of resentment or judgment toward someone else. We may never speak them aloud, but they still carry immense weight in our minds, influencing our behavior and our entire lives:

"No one is ever going to hurt me again!"

"I'll never be like my father!"

"I'll never again let anyone see my true feelings."

"Never again will I have to depend on others!"

Surely, these vows or others like them will sound familiar. As Jesus said, they are evil. They defile us and put us in an evil frame of mind. And as we'll see, often the very things we vow to avoid *occur*—through our own actions or those of others.

Along with the other three components, vows form an important part our internal strongholds. They must be cast down.

OUR BAD PROGRAMMING

Proverbs gives us this valuable insight into human psychology: "...As he thinks within himself, so he is" (Proverbs 23:7). We can begin to see how *what we believe* plays out in our lives. In some ways, our minds are oblivious to age and time. They reach conclusions based on experience, and cling to them regardless of how long ago the experience may have occurred. Like computers, they function according to what has been programmed into them. The flawed, limited information they've absorbed will rule until something new is deliberately introduced.

In the case of Mary that we discussed earlier, her feeling of being unloved infected her life like a computer virus, ruining everything. And like a virus, a lie can lay dormant in our minds for long periods. But a big enough crisis will inevitably trigger it. And it will relentlessly target our actions and thoughts. As Paul stresses, Eve was deceived, and then she transgressed (1 Timothy 2:4). She believed a lie, which led her to sin. Likewise, Mary believes the lie that others don't love her, so when new people walk into her life, she responds accordingly. She'll use the *defensive four*, weapons of unrighteousness, to deal with her pain. These are now her stronghold, which will affect how she sees and responds to every event thereafter. And *every* lie she believes has the potential of developing its own stronghold.

SUMMARY

Jesus came to destroy the works of the enemy, including deception—the lies that are programmed into our minds. Once we're programmed, we use the "defensive four" to protect ourselves from feeling the emotional pain associated with the lies. They become a fortress or prison—a *stronghold*—that is designed to protect us. Later events further validate the lies at the center of the stronghold, and strengthen it.

Every stronghold must be torn down, and the lies replaced with the truth. Jesus told us, "You shall know the truth, and the truth shall set you free" (John 8:32). Jesus Himself *is* the truth, the way and the life (John 14:6). He alone destroys the power of deception and sin, tearing down our strongholds and setting us free.

As we continue, we'll explain how He does this, and how we can experience this truth every day.

CHAPTER EIGHT

Resentment

Follow peace with all men, and holiness, without which no man shall see the Lord: Looking diligently lest any man fail of the grace of God; lest any root of bitterness springing up trouble you, and thereby many be defiled. (HEBREWS 12:14-15).

Bonnie was having problems at her workplace. She had been passed up for a promotion and was in constant conflict with her boss. Over a period of months she became depressed and anxious. As we talked, Bonnie expressed her hurt and anger. She was convinced that her boss and company were to blame, and that she had been mistreated.

I explained that anger is one way we use to deal with pain. Anger can be useful if we're at war, or fighting a bear, but it's not very effective in relationships. When we become angry, our brain releases a chemical which causes us to feel more powerful than we really are. This feeling of power masks our pain. In that sense it is effective, and thus can become addictive. But like anything we become addicted to, the effectiveness wears off and we're left only with bitterness and destruction.

I asked Bonnie what hurt feelings might be hidden underneath her anger. She couldn't answer the question clearly, so I asked it a few more times in different ways, before finally getting a real response. This is normal. Most of us are accustomed to denying our pain. When I counsel people like Bonnie, I normally ask God to show them what they are believing, that is untrue. As Bonnie and I prayed together, we focused on the hurt she felt over being passed up for that promotion. She felt "used," and "belittled."

Her boss made it worse by talking to her in a condescending way. Months had gone by, and she was unable to shake her anger, or as she put it, to "let it go." She felt like quitting, but that prospect would paralyze her with fear. How would she meet her financial needs?

Bitterness can also be described as *unforgiveness*. How does bitterness work in our lives? Let's take an example of a child with his father. If Johnnie feels unloved by his dad, he will erect a wall of bitterness around his heart to protect himself from that pain. If Dad continues his hurtful actions, Johnnie will come to believe that he is permanently unloved and unlovable. And he will go through life interpreting the actions of others based on that presumption. His experience will validate his beliefs. Resentment will become his fortress, the only way he can protect himself. Through repeated experience, he builds his wall higher and thicker till he no longer feels that pain of being unloved—and no one else can penetrate it. This affects Johnnie's lifetime relationships with himself, others, and God.

So how, according to the scriptures, does this root of bitterness, or unforgiveness, cause us trouble? First, unforgiveness is sin, and as such leads inevitably to further sin. The more we resent others the more we will *choose* resentment to deal with our pain. When we allow sin into our Christian lives, it tends to proliferate. But it doesn't stop with us. The Bible tells us that these roots of bitterness *defile many*. The unforgiven traumas from our past come forward into the present, defiling and damaging our relationships with family members, friends, even God.

In Bonnie's case, as she expressed her feeling of being "used," we began to explore prior experiences that might have made her feel that way. Where there is a *fruit*—such as the feeling of abuse Bonnie was experiencing—there is also a *root*. These roots remain active in us until they are specifically removed. The resentment we carry brings the lie from our past forward into the present, defiling our perceptions. Jesus spoke directly to this tendency of sin to obscure our vision:

"Why do you look at the speck of sawdust in your brother's eye and pay no attention to the plank in your own eye? How can you say to your brother, 'Let me take the speck out of your eye,' when all the time there is a plank in your own eye? You hypocrite, first take the plank out of your own eye, and then you will see clearly to remove the speck from your brother's eye" (Matthew 7: 3-5).

A bad tree or root will yield bad, painful fruit. Bitterness is one of the only sins that scripture describes as leading to the *defilement of many*.

I asked Bonnie to recall previous occasions when she had felt *used*. Together, we asked God to reveal it to her. Soon, she was relating several different events. We knew we were getting close to that root. Eventually, she focused on some early experiences involving her stepfather. God was showing her the plank in her eye—the false beliefs that had supported her thinking all these years. When we ask, He is faithful to reveal these things to us.

When we begin this process, the first events that come to our minds are usually the most recent. Those walls we built to protect ourselves also prevent us from seeing what's behind them! We need to tear down the most recent walls to see the ones beyond—those fortresses from our distant past. This is why many of us cannot remember traumatic events that occurred in early childhood. The walls we've erected keep us from seeing them, thereby protecting us from the pain. Each of these past events produces its own pain and resentment, just as each of the lies we believe has its own stronghold.

For Bonnie, the most recent event was this conflict with her company. We asked God to show her any unforgiveness or bitterness she might still be harboring. The spotlight fell on her boss.

"Would you like to forgive him?" I asked. Bonnie had come this far; she wasn't about to turn back now. I led her through a confession, which is the only way to remove the sin of unforgiveness. She prayed in earnest, "Lord, forgive me for my feelings of bitterness towards my boss.

It's important that we take responsibility for our own feelings. We may insist that someone has *made* us feel a certain way, but this is a fallacy. No one can make us feel anything! What Bonnie's boss did was his issue. Bonnie's response was hers, and hers alone. Because of her previous experiences, it was impossible to determine whether her perceptions were valid, or reflected the defilement of earlier resentments. That is the evil of resentment: It distorts the way we see and interpret the actions of others. Jesus understood this human tendency, as he made clear in the passage about removing the planks from our eyes. This is a very important and fundamental truth. As we try to address the problems in our lives, we must first allow God to change our perceptions. Bitterness affects them all, but how?

The human brain is like a computer, programmed by our life experiences. For Bonnie, that included sexual abuse inflicted by her stepfather. He used her for his own gratification. As a result, young, vulnerable Bonnie reached a conclusion about herself: *People use me.* That was now a fixed part of her identity. To deal with the pain of that trauma, she directed bitterness toward both her abuser and herself. She was bitter toward him for obvious reasons, but also blamed herself for allowing it to happen. She actually believed she could have made it stop somehow. This complex of lies was now programmed into her mind and heart. As she grew up and moved on through life, normal events only reinforced it. The programming from her past defiled her perceptions of the present. She saw people as *using* her, even when it was not so. And when someone actually did try to take advantage of her, bitterness, unforgiveness and pain would rise up and cause her to overreact. When we see people responding irrationally to minor offenses, it's usually a sign of this unresolved bitterness rising up from the past.

How could things have worked out differently for Bonnie? Ideally, we should all be trained in the ways of God from childhood. But Bonnie's parents, like all of us, were fallen human beings who had lost the image of God. They couldn't direct her into a healthy life. Not only did they fail to prevent the abuse; when it happened they failed to gently show her that what she had come to believe was not true. They didn't teach her to forgive, and to remove the bitterness in her heart.

This is a typical story, and not just for non-Christian families. The role of Christian parents is to help our children forgive, and teach them to hear the voice of God so they can distinguish between truth and lies. But this is very rarely done. In fact, most of us are never taught to confess our bitterness and unforgiveness towards others.

I often hear people say, "I didn't realize how much resentment I was holding towards this person!" Why is this so common? It's because our sin deceives us. Sin is sneaky. It keeps us in the dark where we can't see. To combat it, we need the help of someone who *can* see. We must develop the habit of *asking* God to search our hearts. He is wonderfully able and willing to do this, as the scripture makes clear:

"In the same way, the Spirit helps us in our weakness. We do not know what we ought to pray, but the Spirit himself intercedes for us with groans that words cannot express. And he who searches our hearts knows the mind of the Spirit, because the Spirit intercedes for the saints in accordance with God's will" (Romans 8;26-27 NIV).

When hurts aren't resolved through forgiveness and truth, they are bound to come forward and defile our current lives. We must deal with these planks in our own eyes before we can see clearly what is happening with others!

Bonnie's abuse at the hands of her stepfather wasn't her only trauma. As we continued to work together, she identified several occasions where she felt used, by boyfriends or family members. She confessed and repented of her resentment toward each one. We also discovered that Bonnie had made a vow to herself never again to allow someone to take advantage of her.

Her stepfather's abuse also made her feel belittled and humiliated. It's no surprise that from then on, she felt belittled by the actions others. This one traumatic event produced a plethora of other lies and roots of bitterness for Bonnie. Where was her mother during this time? Bonnie felt abandoned, unprotected. She tried to tell her mother what had happened, but got no response. No wonder she went through life feeling people *weren't listening* to her! Needless to say, she also felt dirty.

Each lie she was harboring had its root in that one event. And each had to be dealt with separately. That is true for all of us: Each resentment has to be confessed. How many times, you ask? Until all the resentment is gone. Only God knows when that has occurred. Each belief has its own stronghold. As we confess the sin of unforgiveness and bitterness, God forgives us for our unforgiveness! Then, and only then, is forgiveness accomplished. Forgiveness is the removal of *unforgiveness* from our mind and heart. That unforgiveness is itself a sin, and only Jesus can remove sin from us. That's why we cannot forgive as many have told us, by letting the past go, or by forgetting, or simply choosing. Once that sin of unforgiveness is in place, only the blood of Jesus Christ can remove it. This happens when we *confess* it (1 John 1:9).

Once Bonnie confessed and repented of her resentment, the stronghold was torn down. Then we simply asked God to show her the truth about this sense of being "used" by people. God spoke truth to that moment of origin, the earliest event in the chain. He told her something wonderful and gracious: *It was not her fault.* She was just a child! She could not have defended herself or prevented it. Bonnie was set free from the lie through the *truth,* spoken to her by God. She was able to go back to work without the bitterness and hostility in her heart. She no longer felt used. When her boss gave her correction, she received it as just that. He was not trying to belittle her! She no longer needed to quit. Her emotional pain in those two areas was gone.

Bonnie was not healed completely. That's a lifetime project. We all continue to struggle with various lies, and bitter roots throughout our earthly existence. But she was closer to being transformed into the Image of God—that new creature that she is in her spirit. This is the place where we truly are able to worship our Lord.

Being free from our lies and bitterness is a wonderful place to be. I can testify from the experience of my own life. Over a period of years I have received forgiveness in many areas of bitterness, and broken the vows that I made to escape pain. The Lord has been faithful, not just to reveal but to *remove* the lies. I no longer feel self-hatred. I no longer believe that I am *not good enough.* This is just a fraction of the many lies that I believed, and have been delivered from. It is wonderful to be set free from these, but it is more wonderful to have God's way to deal with the continued pain and lies that are revealed through my daily struggle. Many of my relationships have changed. I have become more loving and patient. I am able to forgive so much more easily. I take things less personally. Of course nothing is complete and I am by no means an example of righteousness! But Christ in me is the hope of Glory. He is transforming me, and all of us, into His image and likeness.

The bitter roots we harbor are like viruses, ready to corrupt each aspect of our lives. They must be removed! Until we in the church learn to deal with them in an effective way—God's way—we will not go forward. God has given us the keys. We must be willing to use them.

FORGIVE US OUR DEBTS

When I first began ministering to emotionally wounded people, I found many who simply couldn't forgive those who had wounded them. I'd ask them to pray to forgive their abusers. They would say, "I can't!" At first

Resentment

I thought they were simply unwilling . But I realized later that this was not the case. I began to take a different approach: Encourage people to ask God to forgive *them*. "God, forgive me for holding unforgiveness in my heart!" When they did this, I found that they were immediately able to speak forgiveness toward the other person. They first had to *seek* forgiveness from Christ.

You see, unforgiveness is sin. They could not simply choose to have this sin removed by power of their will. Only Jesus can remove sin—along with its effects on our hearts and minds. As God forgave them their debt of unforgiveness, they were able to then forgive others. It's just as Jesus stated: If we don't forgive others, we probably have not asked for and received forgiveness from Him. And that leaves us in dangerous territory. Those who refuse to take responsibility for their own faults often become Pharisaical, judging others harshly.

Bitterness is unforgiveness. We choose bitterness to keep ourselves from feeling the pain of lies that have been programmed into us, sometimes through our entire lives. Somewhere in our past, we picked up resentment in response to a trauma. The brain, not knowing time or space, then brings this pain and lie forward into all the events of our lives. The bitter root of the past now *defiles many*. Our perceptions are skewed, our thoughts and emotions defiled.

I might be talking to a friend who says something critical. My brain says, "Here we go again! He thinks I'm stupid." But this is perception based on my past programmed beliefs. The problem is that I really believe it!. " Now, I begin to resent my current friend, as I did others in the past. But I can break the chain. Now as a Christian, I have the Holy Spirit in me, convicting me of this bitterness. If I respond to Him, I will immediately confess my resentment.

But I need to do more. I need to look at that thought that popped into my mind and heart: *I am stupid.* I must find where this belief first took hold of my life. God wants to transform my mind (Romans 12:2). This event gives me an opportunity to see my resentment—and be transformed.

Now as I allow the Lord to show me the many events in my life where I believed that I was stupid, I confess my resentment against those that hurt me. In my case, I confessed my resentment towards a family member who had verbally abused me in the past. Then, I asked God to tell me the truth about what I believed. He told me that I was exactly who He created me to be, freeing me from my lie. He brought to my mind a quote from the Psalms: I am fearfully and wonderfully made." This truth set me free. As always, it needed to be applied at the origin of the lie. That's when freedom is lasting.

Roots of bitterness are powerful. Along with the other aspects of the strongholds in us, they keep us from knowing the truth. As we explain in the chapter on *Lies*, we all have been deceived into believing certain things, and cannot behave contrary to our beliefs. We must depend on the Holy Spirit to both convict us, and to show us the lie and the truth. We are helpless without Christ. That is why those who haven't had God's image restored through the new birth cannot experience the healing of Christ. When we reject Christ, there is no hope of having our unforgiveness removed. We may say we forgive others, but true forgiveness can only be accomplished by God—and that only in His redeemed people.

Resentment is one part of the stronghold that must be torn down in our thinking and hearts. Resentment, or unforgiveness is at the foundation of *vows*, and *judgment*, because these came into being only after resentment has taken root. This is another way that resentment defiles, being the instigator of these other attitudes. But just as resentment brings forth the power of the lie, *vows* establish the guarantee of an evil outcome.

CHAPTER NINE

Vows

But I say to you, make no oath at all ...but let your statement be,
'Yes, yes' or 'No, no';
and anything beyond these is of evil. (MATTHEW 5:34, 37)

Being separated from God, we humans have devised a variety of methods to deal with our own sin and pain. One of these is making vows—promises or resolutions that we hope will motivate us to change. We believe that making statements of intent about our lives will somehow alter our behavior, and our destiny. Statements such as, "I'll never let anyone hurt me again," or "I'll never treat my children like my parents treated me," are designed to protect us from the pain we experienced in the past. We use our intellect to deal with things that we can't handle any other way. Will power, hard work and determination become our mantra. And when those don't silence our emotional pain, we seek other alternatives.

But Jesus offers us a very different approach. The book of Romans describes the plight of mankind this way: "They became futile in their speculations, and their foolish heart was darkened" (Romans 1:21). So much for the power of human intellect! Since our minds and hearts are darkened, our attempts to solve our own problems are useless. If we are exceptionally strong-willed, they may work for a time. But eventually they fail. They're like the medications we prescribe for the mentally ill: they don't work for everyone, and even then they only treat symptoms. They can stabilize the patient and ease his pain, but they can't *cure*.

We make vows to ourselves as an expression of resentment. They're our way of responding to the pain others have caused us: parents, friends, lovers, spouses, siblings, bosses, etc. And make no mistake—they are evil. Here are three reasons why:

1. They involve self-protection rather than dependence on God's protection. Anything not done in faith, as the scripture says, is sin. And, "There is a way which seems right to a man, but its end is the way of death" (Proverbs 14:12). Self-protection is a dead-end street. As we regain the image of God, we are to be led by the Spirit of God. He is our only true protection.

2. They're born out of resentment—towards people, God, ourselves. And resentment is sin. Anything arising from it will always defile and poison our future relationships.

3. They place us in prison, and our minds become obsessed with fear. Then, the very thing that we sought to protect ourselves from becomes our reality.

In praying and working with people, I've seen what a powerful impediment to freedom vows can be. They deceive us into believing that we can control our circumstances. If we've determined to do something, then it must happen! If only it were that simple. Can we really stop hurting by declaring, "I refuse to hurt anymore"? We all know the answer to that.

This is the ultimate deception. Like Adam and Eve, we imagine that we can cope with life outside of God's prescribed plan. These vows become our prison, impregnable by any natural power. Like resentment and unforgiveness, they take us captive and bind us.

Let's consider what happens when we make statements like, "I will never be hurt again." We become obsessed with the prospect of being hurt. Our hearts and brains get locked into the fear that, indeed, we *will* be hurt again. That vow does the very opposite of what we intended. This is the evil of the vow. As we walk through life, our brains, like virus-infected computers, react to others in the belief that they will hurt us, even when that is completely untrue. Being "hurt again" becomes the overriding theme of our lives. We see the threat of it everywhere.

We cannot escape this belief on our own. So instead, we do things that seem reasonable to protect ourselves. Some people withdraw from spouses or friends. Others shy away from commitment. We may find ourselves running from relationships before they have a chance to succeed. We may isolate ourselves, or on the other hand, use others to make us feel good about ourselves.

In the case of Ted (in Chapter Six), he interpreted his wife's failure to make him breakfast as an intentional slight. There may have been a thousand explanations for her actions, but almost certainly she wasn't intending to hurt him. No matter. Ted was sure this proved that she didn't love him.

Most of us have had the painful experience of being blamed for things we didn't do. The other person simply overreacted, and no matter how hard we try to make amends, they can't seem to forgive. This is difficult to endure, but it's hard for the person who is overreacting as well. He may be trying to tell himself the truth, reading Bible verses and seeking counsel, but the hurtful belief won't let him go. That is the strength and evil of a vow. Until we discover and dismantle it, it will hold us in its insidious grip. That's how powerful sin is within us. We do what we don't want, and what we *do* want we can't do. As Paul said, "Wretched man that I am! Who will set me free from the body of this death?" (Romans 7:24).

Vows are sin, and they are evil—just as Jesus said.

UNCOVERING THE VOW

Uncovering a vow is usually simple, but not easy. Like the lies we discussed in Chapter Six, vows hide themselves. But like the lies, we can discover them by simply asking. Vows are part of the planks in our eyes—the thinking that supports what we believe about ourselves. As we ask, seek and knock, Jesus will show them to us.

Like lies and resentment, our vows show in what we say. We can learn about ourselves by listening to our own words. But again, the problem is that we've learned *not* to hear our own hearts. We reflexively deny the evil in us. We must practice the art of listening , to God and ourselves, to hear these vows. But the process becomes much easier with practice, as those I work with can testify. As we practice listening and talking with

God, our spiritual hearing becomes more acute. We ask God to show us, and He does.

Another way that we uncover vows is by talking to others about our pain. The issues of our hearts inevitably come out of our mouths, and we will hear those vows. On the other hand, when we're unwilling to face our pain, the vows stay buried. This is why God allows hardship in our lives. Pain forces the dross in our hearts to surface, like the refining process for gold.

This is why scripture talks so much about our need for counsel, confession, and the *people* in the body of Christ. We need to interact. This is the remedy for the inevitable conflicts that occur between people: "If your brother sins (against you), go and tell him his fault between you and him alone. If he listens to you, you have won over your brother" (Matthew 18:15). Why is this so important? It allows the healing process to take place. Meeting together, we find Christ in our midst just as He promised. In that place, prayer and confession accomplish their goals. This explains the current popularity of counseling and support groups. When we do these things, we learn about our hearts.

But learning is one thing; healing and transformation are another. We must rely on Jesus Himself for that work.

We discover our vows by talking, but also by depending on others to listen. This is vital because we've all become expert at *not* hearing our own hearts. We must enlist others to do it for us. As a Christian therapist who deals with people every day, I have developed the ability to hear these things. My clients also have this skill; they can identify the lies, vows, judgment and resentment in themselves, their spouses, family, friends, and neighbors. Submitting to others in this way allows God to work. It's an important part of God's healing work. We need to cultivate open and vulnerable relationships with other believers.

As with the other stronghold components, we uncover our vows by "taking every thought captive to the obedience of Christ" (2 Corinthians 10:5). Again, we must listen to our thoughts and not dismiss them as meaningless. We often ignore our thoughts reflexively because they bring us pain. When a vow or lie comes into our minds, we're apt to deny, dismiss, or replace it with another thought to change the subject.

Consider this vow: "I will never forgive my mom for what she did to me." It's based in real experience and real pain. But I'm an adult now. I like to believe I'm beyond such feelings. So, I wish them away through intellectual gymnastics, telling myself, "Well, my parents are nice now. My mom and I have become best friends." This is my mind's way of overlooking and resisting the pain that the vow was intended to hide. But if it remains unconfessed and unbroken, all kinds of painful consequences can occur. I'll mistrust women. I'll continually misperceive my mother's actions. I'll be unable to forgive others. I will be ever bound to the lie and pain of my mother's actions.

A LIST OF VOWS

It's difficult to compose a list of commonly-held vows, because they often go unrecognized until something painful occurs. As you read through the list below, you'll inevitably recognize some of them. Those you don't recognize may still be present; we all have strong denial mechanisms that help us avoid painful truths. As you read, ask Jesus to reveal which of these may be in you?

- I will never let anyone tell me what to do
- I will never let anyone push me around.
- I won't let people walk all over me.
- I am going to do things on my own.
- I will fight for what I want
- I will be a man.
- I will be good so people will like me.
- I need to make everyone happy.
- I want people to think that I am good.
- I don't want a marriage like my parents.
- I will never be like my father.
- I will never be like my mother.
- I will do everything right so people will love me.
- I won't hurt any more.
- I won't get into another relationship, so I won't get hurt.
- I need others to respect me.
- I'm going to work hard so people will think I'm okay.
- I don't want to hurt my husband (wife).
- I won't treat my children like my parents treated me.
- I have to watch out for myself.
- I won't do anything to get people angry at me.

- I will never cheat on my husband (wife).
- I won't show people that I'm weak.
- I'm never gong to trust anyone again.
- I will never have kids.
- I don't want my children to hurt like I did.
- I won't let anyone else get close to me.
- I will never let myself get out of control.
- I won't let anyone take advantage of me.
- I'll never forgive him for that.
- I must never be alone.
- I need to be perfect.
- I need to avoid conflict at all costs.
- I will never be used again.
- I can't let anyone see me cry.
- I won't cry.
- I will never get divorced.
- I will never abuse my wife.
- I need to be in charge.
- I have to have my freedom.
- I need to make sure that everyone is fine.
- I won't speak up, so I won't feel stupid.
- I'm going to show them that I can do it.
- I won't get close to anyone, so they won't leave me.
- I want our home to be peaceful.
- I won't get close so they won't reject me.
- Sex has to be great.
- I can't live without sex.
- I won't let myself feel pain anymore.
- I don't want my husband (wife) to be mad at me.
- I will never be honest with my parents.
- I'm better off on my own.
- I don't need anyone.
- I have to protect myself from others.
- I don't want to live like this.
- I will not get into trouble.
- I want to be the best.

The first thing you'll notice is that many of these seem to be good things. If I say, "I don't want a marriage like my parents," couldn't that be constructive? The problem is our motivation. If we make such a vow out of judgment or resentment, it is evil.

Vows can surface at any time in our lives. During counseling, clients may reveal vows they've made while telling a story that's totally unrelated. Sometimes, the vows show up at the beginning of the counseling relationship. Other times, they're revealed during a long process.

BREAKING THE VOW

Once we recognize our vows, how can we now rid ourselves of their lasting effects? If we accept that they are evil, we must agree that adopting them was a *sin*. We deal with them as we would any sinful act. We must depend on the blood of Jesus Christ to cleanse us. Only as we confess our sin can He forgive and remove its consequences.

I ask people to simply renounce the vows they have made: "I renounce and break the vow that *I won't be a good mother*." As each vow is uncovered, we do the same thing. It is remarkable to see the understanding and clarity that come to people at this moment. The insight of uncovering the vow brings relief ; they finally understand why they were unable to change. But the *confession* brings freedom. Now, Jesus cleanses them; they no longer need the vow to protect them. Their lives are in His hands.

THE PRICE OF FREEDOM

What are the alternatives to making vows? Simple. Had we been taught the way of Christ, we could have simply asked the Lord to reveal His will. But we tend to be presumptuous, as James points out: "Come now, you who say, 'Today or tomorrow, we shall go to such and such a city, and spend a year there and engage in business and make a profit.' Yet you do not know what your life will like tomorrow. You are just a vapor that appears for a little while and then vanishes away."(James 4:13).

The remedy is to place our lives in God's hands: "Instead, you ought to say, 'If the Lord wills, we shall live and also do this or that'" (James 4:15). He goes on to reiterate Jesus'
warning about making vows: "But above all, my brethren, do not swear, either by heaven, or by earth, or with any other oath; but let your yes be

yes, and your no, no; so that you may not fall under judgment" (James (5:12). What does it mean to say *yes* or *no*, rather than making vows? It simply means accepting reality as it is. We can respond to reality by taking all our thoughts to Jesus, and receiving truth and direction from Him. Instead, most of us resort to the resources of our fallen nature to deal with painful realities.

Freedom comes at a cost. Scripture describes the Christian life as one of suffering and surrender. This is not the way of the flesh; it is and always will be a struggle. But we can be thankful that Christ in us, the hope of glory, helps us. He achieved victory on the cross, and we can too as we abide in Him. Crucifixion is painful. Scripture states that we complete the afflictions of Christ.

But as the Holy Spirit reveals our vows and we renounce them, something happens. Our eyes begin to open, and we see *more* vows. Being freed from one vow allows us to see others. We must not be satisfied with a little gain, when God wants to transform us completely. We must allow Christ to search our hearts daily, to reveal more vows and deception. We must recognize the depth of sin in our flesh, while living in the height of triumph in our spirits.

As I work with people they learn to identify more vows; the process becomes easier. They're more likely to continue the dialogue with Jesus on a continual basis. He is always faithful to reveal the vows in our hearts and minds. We can thank Him for the hardship in our lives, because it reveals our hearts. Then, the peace that passes understanding takes hold of our hearts.

The word often translated "peace" in the Bible also means *to join with*. Jesus joins with us in our pain, crucifying that which binds us—the vows we have made. He then resurrects us into His glorious freedom

CHAPTER TEN

Judgment

Judge not, that you be not judged. For with the judgment you pronounce you will be judged, and with the measure you use it will be measured to you. Why do you see the speck that is in your brother's eye, but do not notice the log that is in your own eye? Or how can you say to your brother, 'Let me take the speck out of your eye,' when there is the log in your own eye? You hypocrite, first take the log out of your own eye, and then you will see clearly to take the speck out of your brother's eye.

(MATTHEW 7:1-29; ESV)

Denise was having trouble with her son. Daniel was 16 now, and seemed to be getting more rebellious by the day. He was often in trouble at school, and had become a habitual liar. The more he disobeyed her, the more frustrated she became. As he entered adolescence their relationship had spiraled downward, and she often found herself shouting at him. By the time she came to me for counseling, she was desperate.

"I've tried everything," She fumed. "He never listens to me! I know he's doing this to me on purpose."

This last sentence was key. She was convinced Daniel was *intentionally* lying and refusing to listen. And he was *doing this to her*. Instead of seeing a troubled young man who needed help, Denise had personalized his behavior and drawn conclusions.

Denise had formed a *judgment* of her son.

Judgment occurs when we form conclusions about others based on false information, or our own bitterness. It's not an assessment of the person's actions, but a verdict on *whom* and *what* they are. In this situation, Denise had developed bitterness in her heart towards her son. And it led her to conclude that he was deliberately tormenting her.

We've already noted Jesus' admonition about judging: The way we judge others is the way we will be judged. And we've seen his shrewd insight into human nature when he told us to remove the plank in our own eye so we could see clearly the speck in our brother's. As we've made clear, the *plank* in our eye is often the beam that holds our structure of false beliefs in place.

Could these two passages refer to the same thing? When we judge others, we reflect what is inside us. We must therefore be willing to examine our own beliefs and thinking (planks) before we can accurately see what is in the other person.

When Daniel dismissed his mother's words, her brain would tell her, "There he goes again. He just won't listen. He's doing this to you intentionally!" But how could she know that? Denise needed to examine what was in her own eye—her own thoughts and beliefs. When she finally did, the result was very revealing.

The belief that "no one listens to me" had been a theme in Denise's life long before her troubles with her son. In fact, it had shown up in many of her relationships. As we talked, we discovered that this belief was programmed into her from childhood. She now projected it onto Daniel. To be sure, he had often disobeyed and refused to listen—as teenage boys are apt to do. But, instead of forgiving him, Denise took his actions as a validation of what she already believed: *No one listens to me.*

This is what happens when lies go unhealed. In this light, the words of Jesus take on greater depth: The way to recognize lies we have believed is to observe how we judge others. When we take the actions of other people personally, it's a good sign that we're judging them, out of our own pain, resentment and strongholds.

Denise was finally willing to confess her resentment and judgment toward Daniel. This gave her a whole new perspective: Daniel's actions were about him, not her. When she resented and judged him, she made it about her. It then became her issue. This clouded her perception of her son. The plank in her eye was preventing her from seeing clearly the speck in his

As you can see, these scriptures from the Sermon on the Mount are critically important for true healing. We must always be willing to look at ourselves before we can ever understand others. Denise asked her son for forgiveness, and opened her heart to him once more. And she began to look at the strongholds she had formed around her wounds and false beliefs.

Like the other defense mechanisms we've discussed, judgment is really a device our minds use to keep us from seeing our own issues. But this is sin! Denise, instead of recognizing her own lie, accused her son. He was *making her feel that way*. When we say things like this, we reveal our own beliefs. If I say, "You make me feel stupid," that's a sign that *I believe I am stupid*. But instead of facing my belief, I judge and blame you. Psychology refers to this as *projection* or *transference*.

Judgment forms another part of the stronghold, gripping us in its claws, entrapping us in its lies.

In that same Sermon on the Mount, Jesus says, "Do not give what is holy to dogs, and do not throw your pearls before swine, lest they trample them under their feet, and turn and tear you to pieces" (Matthew 7:6). This passage take on added significance in light of the ones we've just cited. When people are unwilling to see the truth, especially regarding what is in them, they can become brutish, irrational and aggressive—like swine. If you try to show it to them, they can tear you to pieces! They will blame you for their pain, and treat you like the perpetrator. And they'll say with great conviction, "You made me feel this way!" We've all known people who can't take responsibility for their own feelings—always blaming others, always playing the victim. We all have a little victim in us.

If Denise had continued to blame her son, she would have torn him to pieces with her blame, anger and resentment. In fact, this is what she was already doing. Certainly, Daniel was responsible for his own actions. He needed someone to *speak the truth in love* to him. But as long as Denise harbored judgment in her heart, she could never do that. Denise wasn't just judging her son. There were other people from her past whom she had never forgiven. When she judged Daniel harshly, that unresolved resentment was rising to the surface. After she finally confessed and received healing, her relationship with Daniel began to look very different. She saw that, many times, *she* had helped precipitate their confrontations. And she finally recognized that he had his own pain. It wasn't all about her.

At this point, she brought Daniel into my office. To her surprise, he quickly responded to the Holy Spirit. Their reconciliation had begun.

Here are some things to look for regarding judgment:

- If we treat the actions of others as personal attacks, we're probably guilty of judging. When Daniel lied to his mother, that was his own issue. Her pain, in response, was hers. Even if he *intentionally* lied, it was not inevitable that she would feel pain. The lying triggered something already in her mind and heart. She then labeled her son: *Liar! He never listens*! She had now crossed over into judgment. Paul assures us, "No temptation has overtaken you but such as is common to man" (1 Corinthians 10:13). We all have a carnal nature which protects itself from its own pain by sinning against others. Often, people's sin is just that—a way to protect themselves from the pain caused by others. Jesus showed us the way out—forgive. How often? "Seventy times seven" (Matthew 18:22). In other words, without limit.

- Follow the pain. If there is any pain associated with a memory, that's a sign that there may be judgment there too. It may even be justified according to the circumstances, but it's still sin, and will cripple us. We must allow God to remove all judgment and resentment to receive our healing.

- When we form a judgment toward someone else, it usually relates to a similar painful belief in us. This is the concept of *fruit* and *root*. What we experience now points to a root that was planted earlier. We must remove the root from the past before we can accurately see the present. The other person may not be completely responsible for the emotional pain we're feeling. Most likely they are not! If we don't look inside and find a way to forgive, we'll be forever bound, unable to confess and therefore unable to receive forgiveness. Jesus said, "For if you forgive men when they sin

Judgment

against you, your heavenly Father will also forgive you. But if you do not forgive men their sins, your Father will not forgive your sins" (Matthew 6:14-15).

- If we are *mind-reading*, we're probably committing the sin of judgment. This occurs when we believe we heard something that the other person never verbalized. Our minds tend to hear what they already believe. I might tell my wife Sandra, "The lasagna was a little overcooked tonight." But what she hears might be, "You can't do anything right!" She's mind-reading. We judge and resent other people for things they never said. This is a hard one to deal with, because in our deception we truly believe what we thought we heard. And if we don't trust the other person, we may never be willing to believe what they say. It is important to follow scripture on this point: "If a brother or sister sins, go and point out the fault, just between the two of you. If they listen to you, you have won them over" (Matthew 18:15). Because our perceptions are so unreliable, it's important to go to the other person for feedback. Regarding the lasagna, if I'm wise, I'll approach my wife and say, "Honey, that wasn't what I meant at all!" And I'll pray that she's willing to believe me. If I listen to her response, I may hear the belief in her heart.

Ted was an attorney with a thriving practice, who had done very well for himself. His first marriage failed, but he remarried and brought his new wife, Barbara, and her 13 year-old son into his home. Initially, Ted kept their bank accounts together, but soon found that his wife had made some foolish purchases. He took away her credit cards and separated the bank accounts. Barbara was working, but made far less money than Ted. The tension between them grew. After just three years of marriage, Barbara was ready to leave.

Ted's feelings were clear: He was being "taken advantage of" by his wife and stepson. She constantly complained about money, but he was providing for all their needs. When he gave her some freedom with the credit cards, she ran the balances to the limit. She wasn't respecting how hard he worked to support them.

Barbara, on the other hand, freely admitted that she had problems with money. Spending made her feel good abut herself. She too had been married before. It was an abusive marriage, and she dealt with her pain by accumulating things. She acknowledged her weakness to Ted and apologized repeatedly. But nothing she did ever seemed "good enough" for him.

I explained to them how judgment works. Ted finally saw the lie he had believed: *People take advantage of me.* This was in place long before he met Barbara. Now he was judging her for doing the very same thing. His sinful, judgmental attitude was keeping them from experiencing the relationship they both hoped for.

It turned out, this belief had a very powerful root in a childhood trauma. Ted's father had molested him when he was young. This led to a permanent feeling of being taken advantage of, as well as being disrespected. Ted asked God—and Barbara—to forgive him for his judgmental spirit. He renounced the vow that "no one would ever take advantage of him again." And he confessed the judgmental attitude that was part of the stronghold in his life.

Meanwhile, Barbara confessed her habit of using spending to make herself feel good. She also began to look at her responses to Ted. He would often withdraw emotionally, and she took that as a signal that she "wasn't good enough."

"Did he ever actually *say* that?" I asked her.

"Well, he never used those words."

We began to explore the previous experiences that would have produced this feeling in Barbara. There were plenty. Beyond her first husband, Barbara had been involved with several boyfriends who treated her cruelly. But behind all that was a very abusive father. To make matters worse, Barbara's mother let her know that her father had wanted to abort her. Talk about not being good enough! Barbara's lie and wound were deep. But by confessing her resentment toward Ted and the others, she finally found freedom. She asked God and Ted for forgiveness.

Ted and Barbara's healing is a work in progress. Through prayer, confession and continual reliance on the Holy Spirit, they have each confronted their issues. Ted no longer fears being taken advantage of. God told him that He'll always protect him; Ted can depend on God for everything. And Barbara no longer believes she's not good enough. She heard God tell her something precious: She's made in His image, and she is His princess.

That's what makes it all worthwhile.

CHAPTER ELEVEN

Vain Imaginations

Casting down imaginations, and every high thing that exalteth itself against the knowledge of God, and bringing into captivity every thought to the obedience of Christ.
(2 CORINTHIANS 10:5; KJV)

Because that, when they knew God, they glorified him not as God, neither were thankful; but became vain in their imaginations (reasoning), and their foolish heart was darkened.
(ROMANS 1:21)

How many times have you found yourself trying to undo the past? If you kept track, you might be surprised; most of us do it quite often. When we tune in to what we actually say through the course of a day, we find we're constantly making statements about past events—and future ones we hope will occur.

I should have ...

I wish ...

If only ...

What I need to do is ...

Next time, I'll ...

Often in counseling, I hear people describe the horrible things that have happened to them, and then conclude with words like those above. They lost all power and control in a traumatic event, but they imagine that by doing things differently, they could have changed it all. This is a great example of a *vain imagination*. Such flights of fancy are comforting, but they only bring us into further bondage.

Have you ever listened to yourself talk? As we've mentioned, it can be very revealing. You'll probably find that you indulge in these vain imaginations on a daily basis. These are *things we tell ourselves* to manage our emotional pain. It's our intellect's way of trying to fix or change the past.

Let's look at some examples.

I had been counseling Alice for several weeks. She was just beginning to recognize some of the walls of resentment she had erected. As things became clearer, we began to identify her incorrect ways of dealing with pain—such as her habit of telling herself *what she should have done:*.

"He made me angry again, and I yelled at him. I should have just walked away, shouldn't I?"

She doesn't realize that this is a vain imagination. It's not grounded in reality. Saying, "I should have walked away" is futile, simply because it's not what actually happened. What Alice needed to do was face reality. What made her so angry? What feelings had her husband touched on? Why did she feel he didn't love her? These were the questions her behavior was trying to raise, and instead she wished them away with "I should have …"

That is what these imaginations are in essence—wishful thinking. And we all engage in them to one degree or another. We use them to trick our minds into thinking that all is well.

But it's not.

In Alice's case, she had learned to respond to traumatic situations intellectually, by figuring out the *right* thing to do. In this case that would have meant walking away—or so she imagines. But reality is, she didn't walk away. She felt unloved by her husband, and retaliated. This could have been a valuable moment, showing Alice what was deep in her heart—her belief that she was *unloved*. But the pain of that lie was too great to deal with. So instead, she protected herself.

This was her way of rationalizing her feelings; a way to make sense of them without the work of the cross. It reflected the delusion that she *really could* figure things out on her own. And rather than taking responsibility for her feelings, she blamed her husband. This allowed her to deflect her pain and deny the state of her own heart.

We come back to the admonition of Jesus: "First take the plank out of your own eye …"

There were lies in Alice's heart that she needed to face. Her vain imaginations were simply helping her avoid that. But there was more. As we continued to talk, she realized that she had married a man who tends to lie to protect himself. Her response was rueful: "I wish I never married him!" At other times, she exclaimed, "I should have never put myself in this situation."

Wishing is yet another vain imagination, grounded in unreality. And it doesn't help at all. It's another way of denying the truth and avoiding the pain of what we believe. In Alice's case, this was understandable, because she truly believed that things were *hopeless*. Her mind had been programmed with the notion that she was unloved, and her husband's continual lying only reinforced that belief. There seemed to be no way out.

But of course, there was. Alice could have recognized her pain as something originating in herself. That would enable her to stop judging her husband. And she could take ownership of this belief that she was unloved. Where did it come from? Most certainly, it was some set of events that happened long before she met her husband. This would have fulfilled Jesus' admonition to *look at the plank in our own eye*. But her continual wishing allowed her to put that off and avoid responsibility.

Alice expressed another wish, which all of us are familiar with: *If only…* "If only Jim would truly love me, I'd feel better." This kind of imagination subtly allows us to depend on our own thoughts to control things, rather than bringing them to the living God for consolation and truth. Sometimes, *if only* works—for awhile. Alice may have been able to convince her husband to change; stop lying, start being kind and considerate. She would have felt better, but only until the next time he slipped up. Then, she'd be miserable again. Until Alice knew deep in her spirit that God *loves* her, any solution would only be temporary.

Wishing things were different is a backhanded way of justifying our mistakes. Another deceit is to imagine that with the new insight we've found, we could have done things better. The common thread in all these examples is that they represent attempts to deal with pain through our intellect. But as you may have noticed, we can't really control emotions with our intellect! And when we try, we miss out on God's healing. The first step in that process is to allow ourselves to feel all the pain we've been trying to push away, and then let God show us where it's coming from. Then, we depend on Him to speak truth into our minds, setting us free.

As we've seen, our actions stem from what we believe about ourselves and the world. Many of these beliefs are lies, not based in the truth. So we must be changed inside before our behavior and feelings can change—not the other way around, as some people insist. Simply telling ourselves what we must do won't work. The apostle Paul understood our predicament, lamenting, "I have the desire to do what is good, but I cannot carry it out. For what I do is not the good I want to do; no, the evil I do not want to do-this I keep on doing" (Romans 7:18-19). This is the power of sin in us. Sin and deception reign in our mortal bodies. To experience God's transforming work, we must tear down our strongholds of sin and lies. The intellectual manipulations we've described here only support our minds in their deception.

SOME POPULAR *VAIN IMAGINATIONS:*

- I should have...
- I wish I had...
- If only...
- Next time I'll...
- I didn't mean to...
- I really didn't want to.....
- It's not fair...
- I didn't know.....
- No one told me...

THE VAINEST OF THE VAIN

What is the biggest vain imagination of them all? Let me digress for a moment with the lyrics to an old Doris Day song:

Que sera, sera
Whatever will be, will be
The future's not ours to see
Que sera, sera.

What does this have to do with our subject? Well, as I often tell friends and clients, *we don't know what healing looks like*. How could we? We've never experienced it before! Our minds are under the power of deception. We're all born in sin, with false beliefs programmed into us from conception. It's impossible for us to imagine what we've never experienced or felt. When we try, it only reflects our faulty beliefs.

So what do we do? We attempt to act out what we think it might *look like* if we were healed. We imagine the feelings we would have, and try to get those feelings. We tell ourselves—to borrow the theme from another popular song—"Get happy!" Behave as if you've already been healed! We observe how others act—in the mistaken belief that they know something we don't—and try to mimic their behavior.

We'll do anything to avoid the hardship, pain and battle of dealing with what's inside us. But all this is vain. How can we receive the fruit of healing without being healed? We cannot imitate the work of Christ in us. And other people are no help in this matter. Since I don't know your heart or see your experiences, I can't give you a roadmap. I can share what God has done in me. But only Christ can lead you there. Even the apostle Paul, who encouraged believers to follow his example, said in a candid moment that he had not yet attained his goal. As always, we must look to Christ alone.

The New Testament contains many directions about how we should behave. But are these meant as rules—or as pictures of what maturity looks like? They show us what it means to be healed, spiritual and Christ-like, since we're incapable of seeing it in our present state. When Paul says, "Husbands, love your wives as Christ loves the church and gave himself for her," I might be tempted to throw my hands up in despair: I can't do that! It's not in me! Of course, I can't—not without being transformed. But when I see my inability and sin in this regard, God can cleanse and transform me. Then, anything is possible.

So, what is the biggest vain imagination? Just this: We confuse doing what we *think* is right, with letting Christ manifest His rightness in us. We attempt to be what we have not yet attained. We depend on programs, principles, and *doing the right thing* to get us where we want to be—instead of sitting at Christ's feet until He brings the changes in us. God sees our hearts; only He knows the changes we really need. If we submit to his daily transformation, He will instill a new set of behaviors in us, and we will manifest His glory. Then, as Paul said, "It is no longer I who live, but Christ lives in me" (Galatians 2:20).

Then why does Paul tell us how to behave? *Husbands, love your wives; wives, respect your husbands. Be humble. Bear each other's burdens. Pray without ceasing. Love one another.* I believe Paul is painting a picture of what true healing will look like when we are transformed by Christ. We cannot love as Christ does until He transforms us. If we are truly doing these things, it is because Christ has changed our hearts. Our own efforts to approximate them will always be self-righteous—marked not by love, but manipulation, control and legalism.

Attempting to live as if we had attained, when we haven't, is a vain imagination—the biggest vain imagination of them all! These things take time. The apostles sat at Jesus' feet for three years. The new Church in Jerusalem sat at the apostles' feet for many years after that. Christ was forming Himself in His people as they lived with one another; iron sharpening iron. The Holy Spirit was transforming a motley band of misfits into the body of Christ.

It's instructive to look at the story of Ananias and Sapphira in the book of Acts. They were members of the church, but they lied about their true behavior and intent. They saw everyone around them pitching in to sustain the new work God was doing. They too sold a property they owned, and contributed the proceeds to the church—but kept back part of it. Then, they lied about it. God didn't appreciate that—and took their lives.

Were they indulging in this greatest of vain imaginations? Were they simply trying to look good? Was their behavior so different from ours? They may also have been motivated by fear when they held back part of their money—fear of not having enough. Most of us can relate to that. I certainly can! But why would God *kill* them? Maybe the damage they would have caused this young body of believers was too great. God has his purposes; we can only believe He acted in the best interest of the church. But it's a strong warning about trying to mimic God's work without receiving his transformation.

People often come to me saying, "I want to learn to communicate with my spouse." But they may not be ready for God's transforming work: revealing their hearts, tearing down their old patterns, crucifying their flesh. Our natural minds always seek comfort and ease, as our vain imaginations reveal. We place our interests before those of others. We love those who love us, and despise those who don't. Paul spoke of people who would *have a form of godliness, but deny the power thereof*. Doesn't that describe all of us to some extent? Thank God, He no longer condemns us for our sin. We can't change ourselves, but by confessing and casting down our vain imaginations, we can see Christ exalted in our lives.

So, when Alice asks, "What do I do to get my husband to love me?" my response is, "Let the Lord change you first." "What about when he gets angry? What do I do then?" Same thing: Let God remove the resentment, vows and sin in your life. That's what is defiling your relationship. Then, you'll see clearly the speck in your brother's (or husband's) eye. Then, and only then, will God be able to manifest His unconditional love in you.

"But," you may ask, "What is so wrong with wanting to plan what to do next? Isn't that a good thing?"

It might seem good. But how can we plan what we'll do in the future if we've only reacted negatively in the past? This is a common mistake. We plan what we'll say or do, how we'll react to some event in the future. Based on my experience as a counselor, this is a sure recipe for failure. It's always a mistake to bet on our own performance.

Then when we fail, it reinforces our sense of helplessness and inadequacy. The thoughts in our heads, the words in our mouths, and the actions we engage in reflect what is in our hearts. God uses these things to point out our issues and lies. When we do anything other than allow ourselves to be who we really are, we cut off this important avenue of God's dealing. These lies, as we've shown, lead to sin. Since Jesus paid the price for our sin, we don't suffer under God's condemnation. So, sin and pain now are important ways that we can recognize deceptive thinking.

As most of have experienced, when we attempt to stop sinning, it only comes back with a vengeance. That is why it is so important that we forgive one another. We all need a safe, supportive climate where we can reveal our failings without fear of condemnation. Only then can we share the depths of our hearts. That is what Christ did for us when He put us in a place of justification before God. Our lives are hidden in Him.

God wants that same security to exist in our relationships with each other. We must trust God to work through our brothers and sisters as we restore and encourage each other. This is a particular challenge for husbands and wives, who live with their partners' most intimate faults. Especially in marriage, we need to support and challenge one another even as our sin and deception are being revealed. Are you expecting too much of your spouse? Do you demand perfection? This, too, is vain imagination!

When we finally confess and cast down our vain imaginations, we surrender, placing ourselves at the feet of Jesus our Lord and Savior. We experience His mercies new every morning. This is when we see our behavior change, our hearts made pure, and our minds transformed. Now we can finally love as the scriptures say. How did Jesus say the world would know His disciples? By our love for each other. May we all experience this in its fullness.

The process of transformation is mysterious. None of us can see what we will be—or ought to be. I have ministered to many addicts who love God, yet still remain bound by their addictions. Does this mean God is not active in their lives? A common lie is that if someone is destitute, he must not be in God's will. The deception of the enemy is great. But would God really leave a child of His in deception? Is Christ any more less Christ if His children suffer? Of course not. That is why we are to love, not condemn, one another.

Vain Imaginations

We are all part of His body. If it pleased God to wound His own Son, then we should expect to be bruised as well. But when I am bruised, doesn't it prove to all the great cloud of witnesses, and all the principalities and powers that God can keep His own, no matter what? He is able to keep us from the enemy. Greater is He in us than he that is in the world. God's ways are higher than our ways. It is vain imagination to believe that God is not manifest in His people, even through their temporal suffering. For the reward set before Him Jesus endured the cross, taking on Himself the sin of the world. Won't we also receive a reward as we persevere in suffering? Some believers can't imagine living without physical comforts. But it is a vain imagination to believe that we should all be rich, or without pain, struggle and conflict. We do not seek comfort, but we seek the God who is our comforter. This is *not* vain.

We should cease trying to be what we are not. The scriptures say we have been made the righteousness of God through our confession of faith and dependence on Christ. A bird cannot swim like a fish. And we cannot change our sinful ways. When we see things in our lives that violate God's word, we can only acknowledge them as places that need to be transformed. We can bring our thoughts captive to the obedience—attentive listening—of Christ. This has nothing to do with denying the wrong things in us, and trying harder to do right. We can't accomplish it through our own resources. Our strength, will power, understanding and intellect are all useless in this endeavor. Rather, we confess—agree with God—that these things exist, and cast ourselves on His mercy

WHAT TO DO?

As we begin to pay attention to our words, thoughts and behavior, we'll find that much of our talk is consumed with vain imaginations. I use the word *consumed*, because we tend to spend inordinate amounts of time thinking about them, analyzing them, or rationalizing them—rather than simply asking God for the truth. In that light, it's a miracle that these habits can ever change. Of course, it only happens through the Holy Spirit in us.

So, what are we to do? Ask God. Then, listen to Him. Wait on Him for an answer. And when He answers, respond. He tells us the Truth. That Truth may come in the form of conviction of sin, or through a blessed release. But it is always the Holy Spirit.

We must:

- Stop depending on vain imaginations to relieve our pain. They can't.

- Listen to our hearts, confess, and ask the Lord's forgiveness.

- Ask Him to show us *why* we are using vain imaginations.

He is faithful. When we ask, He shows us the emotional pain we are desperately trying to protect ourselves from. In most cases, once we confess and ask Jesus to show us the Truth, He will reveal our resentment towards someone who has hurt us. Once we confess that resentment, Jesus will often show us the lie that is at the root of our emotional pain.

CHAPTER TWELVE

Victim

Why do you look at the speck that is in your brother's eye, but do not notice the log that is in your own eye? Or how can you say to your brother, 'Let me take the speck out of your eye,' and behold, the log is in your own eye? You hypocrite, first take the log out of your own eye, and then you will see clearly to take the speck out of your brother's eye. Do not give what is holy to dogs, and do not throw your pearls before swine, or they will trample them under their feet, and turn and tear you to pieces.

(MATTHEW 7:3-6)

In this extraordinary passage, Jesus Christ refers to people as "swine" and "dogs!" What would cause Him to use such harsh language? This verse can be difficult to understand, but it begins to make sense when we consider it in relation to the previous verses. There, Jesus exhorts each of us to look first at the beam or log in our own eye—which we've described as the structure that supports our false beliefs. Could a *dog* in this context refer to someone who refuses to look at himself before he judges another? And, could a *swine* be the person who continually finds the faults in others, while being oblivious to his own?

It's interesting to note what happens when we try to share valuable insights with these "swine:" They will turn on us, Jesus said, and tear us to pieces. This is actually a common phenomenon, known in psychology as the *victim triangle*. It's not so surprising that Jesus described this human behavior two thousand years ago.

The Victim Triangle

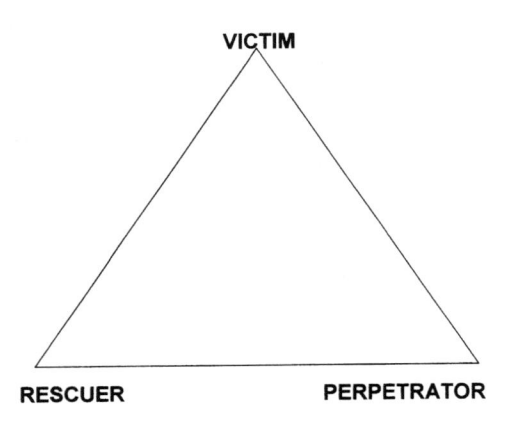

```
           VICTIM


RESCUER         PERPETRATOR
```

We must be clear: The *victim* we refer to here is not a true victim, such as someone who has experienced a molestation or attack. Rather, we're dealing with the kind of person Jesus described: someone who refuses to take responsibility for his feelings and actions, and habitually blames others for how he feels. Most of us have encountered people like this. But we've also done these things ourselves. This is very common behavior, dating back to the original sin when Adam and Eve pointed the finger at each another—and God.

What do we mean by not *taking responsibility* for our actions? An example from a therapy session will illustrate: Alex borrowed a small sum of money from Gina and didn't pay it back as promised. In relating the story, Gina said she felt "used" and "taken advantage of." This was a personal assault upon *her*. She now occupied the place of the *victim* on the triangle above. She was feeling pain due to her belief.

But according to Jesus, before Gina can judge Alex she must first examine herself. Was this belief somehow already in her heart and mind, having been programmed there earlier in her life? She must take responsibility for her beliefs and feelings. When Alex broke his promise, that was *his* sin. Gina's feelings belong to her. Acknowledging this is an important part of breaking out of the *victim mentality*.

Are you playing the role of victim? There are ways to tell. One of the signs: You tend to take things personally. Rather than seeing other people's behavior as *their* issue, you internalize it as a personal assault. Your battle cry is *"You made me feel this way!"*

Gina not only blamed Alex for not paying her, but took it a step further, blaming him for her feelings. Now, Alex was the perpetrator, she was his victim. In keeping with the dynamics of the *victim triangle*, she must now find someone or something to rescue her. In this case, Gina went to her friend Jane. She tried to enlist Jane against Alex, portraying him as the problem, and soliciting sympathy for her own feelings. She was unwilling to accept that her feelings of *being used* belonged to her. In fact, this was almost certainly not the first time she had felt this way.

According to scripture, when conflicts arise we should go to the other person and make it right. This would include checking to see what the person really meant by their actions. In Alex's case, he might really have intended to pay Gina, but couldn't.

It didn't matter. The victim blames, regardless of objective facts. That includes blaming others for one's own feelings—even if the person did nothing to cause them. This was what happened in Gina's case. When Jane refused to align with her against Alex, Gina felt rejected, and blamed Jane for making her feel that way. It seemed that everyone was against her now. Jane had now assumed the role of *perpetrator*.

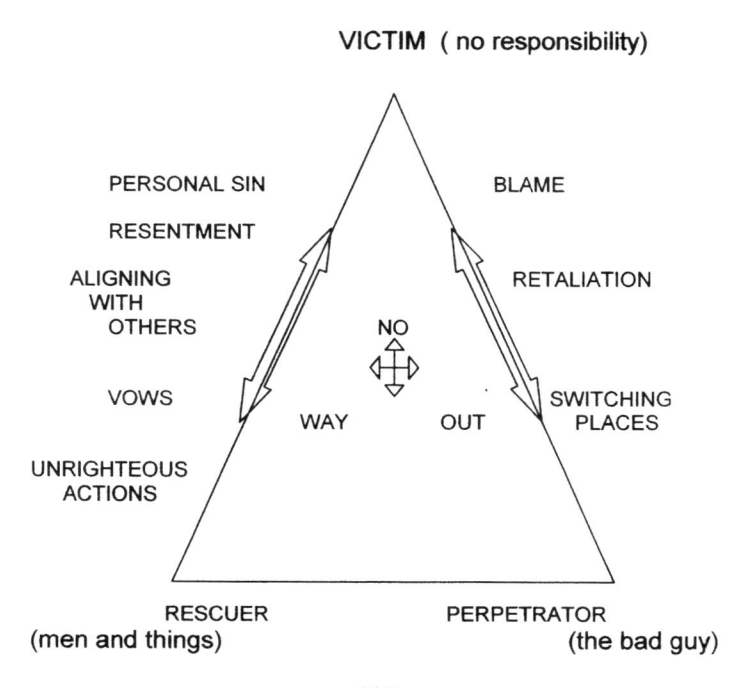

VICTIM (no responsibility)

PERSONAL SIN

RESENTMENT

ALIGNING WITH OTHERS

VOWS

UNRIGHTEOUS ACTIONS

NO WAY OUT

BLAME

RETALIATION

SWITCHING PLACES

RESCUER
(men and things)

PERPETRATOR
(the bad guy)

Gina resorted to various means to rescue herself from her pain: gossip, overeating, drug abuse—anything that might help her feel good. She began to tear Jane and Alex to pieces with her backbiting, anger and hatred. One of the consequences of this rampage of blame was impaired judgment: Gina could no longer discern reality from falsehood. We have all fallen prey to this scenario: people who overacted to something we said or did, or who accused us of being like their mom or dad. It has no relationship to reality, but the person genuinely believes it.

This is how it goes, according to the triangle. I feel used by a friend. Then, unwilling to take responsibility for that feeling, I blame him. He becomes the perpetrator, or bad guy. If he doesn't agree with me, I look for someone or something to rescue me. I might call on another friend to validate my plight, or tell myself, "See? You just can't trust people."

Then I take the next corner of the triangle. If my friend doesn't rescue me out of my feelings, I begin to resent him, which often leads to gossip and slander. I either withdraw my love, or attack him. Notice, I have now changed my position on the triangle and become the perpetrator. My "friend" becomes my victim.

Ultimately, the person who does not take responsibility for his actions or feelings will become a perpetrator—turning on his victim, as Jesus said, and tearing him to pieces.

But if a person really does sin against me, isn't it realistic to feel used? My answer may surprise you: No. His offense is his own issue. God simply tells me to forgive. But the offending actions now reveal something in me: my belief that "people use and take advantage of me." If the belief did not exist, neither would the feeling. I could simply have recognized the offense as the other person's issue, and dealt with it as such.

Unfortunately, most of us don't follow the scriptures in these situations. We don't go to each other in love to resolve issues. Instead, we play the victim card and look for someone or something to rescue us from our pain. Then, we blame the person for our feelings.

In many marriages, it's common for the husband and wife to continually switch places on the triangle. First, he attacks her in anger, blaming her for his feeling. He's not being listened to, or respected. Then she feels unloved, and blames him for "making me feel that way." She withdraws her love—making him the victim again. Now, both are victims in their own eyes, and both see the other as the perpetrator. The dance goes on and on. Dad (or Mom) might bring in a son or daughter to rescue or agree with him; to validate that he has every right to blame *her*.

But he doesn't.

We must each take full responsibility for what we feel. No one makes us feel anything. Whatever someone else might do to us, it is what we believe about that event which causes our feeling. That is why we are told to forgive quickly. Love covers the multitude of sins—and it is not easily offended.

We typically do the triangle dance over and over, entering into different triangular relationships with various people—sometimes with several people at the same time. But Jesus is clear: If we do not look at the plank in our eye first, we cannot see clearly what's in others lives, let alone our own. We will play the role of victim and perpetrator, blaming others and looking for rescue from our emotional pain.

If the other person doesn't rescue us as we ask, we will then feel victimized, make her the villain, and then turn around and mistreat *her*. The triangle is endless, and it wreaks havoc in our relationships.

We can even play the victim with ourselves. And the results are just as destructive. As we've explained, sin is our way of dulling the pain, rather than dealing with it. In this scenario, we're using drugs, sex, alcohol, or anger to rescue us. We can even use work or religious activity in this way. These things become easy solutions, enabling us avoid feeling our pain or looking at our beliefs. If someone happens to get in the way of our self-rescuing—by asking us to stop drinking, not agreeing, or not consenting to sex—we get angry and become perpetrators ourselves.

Many marriages are based on one partner trying to make the other happy. And many parent-child relationships work this way too: The parent expects her child to perform perfectly. The child learns, *If I don't make Mom feel good, I am bad, and I will be victimized.* The child decides to rescue Mom by always making her happy: *If I rescue her, she will love me.* The dance goes on.

This triangle plays out in every relationship in this life. We all have some of this behavior in us, because we all have sin in our flesh, and our minds need to be transformed. By identifying how we play into this triangle, we can see where we've been judging, resenting, accusing, and otherwise sinning against ourselves and others.

What is the way out of the triangle? First, it's not enough just to see our part in it. Mere intellectual understanding can never free us from the grip of these actions. But as we see, and confess to God, He can set us free. The way out of the triangle is through God. We must recognize that God alone can comfort us in our pain. He alone can validate and rescue us. Looking to other humans for this is useless—other than for temporary pleasure. When we form "rescuing" relationships with anyone but God, they become addictive. We must continue to get the other person to rescue us again and again, using any ungodly tactics at our disposal.

To get out of the triangle we must take captive our false belief, recognize it as our own, and go to Christ with that pain. We then hear Him tell us the truth about the incident, and we can forgive. We recognize that in Christ we have all things, and therefore, are never without. No one can use us, because in love all is freely given. Instead of attacking others, we forgive unconditionally. With God's help, we step out of the triangle.

We can do nothing except ask God to reveal to us where we are in this with others. Once we see ,we can now confess our issues before God. As we begin to see more clearly, we recognize the ways we attempt to rescue, be rescued, blame, or avoid responsibility for our feelings. This is crucial. When I explain this triangle to people, they invariably recognize its simplicity, but also its basis in reality. They can usually see themselves in every part of the triangle.

When Bob married Jane, he brought his 12 year-old daughter Stacey from a previous marriage, who visited every other weekend. Jane didn't have any children, but after several months, she noticed behaviors in Stacey that concerned her. She approached Bob, who immediately became defensive. Bob had long felt like a failure as a father and a person. He couldn't face the guilt he felt over his divorce. As Jane tried to be a good stepmother, Bob became less open to her opinions and eventually began to withdraw from her. He blamed her for meddling, and accused her of telling him he wasn't a good father; he just wasn't good enough. This seemed bizarre to Jane, because she had never used these words. As Bob withdrew further and further, she began to feel he wasn't listening and didn't love her. She wanted him to rescue her from these feelings, so she continued to pressure him. When that didn't work, she blamed him, enlisting her friends for support and validation. She would talk about Bob and solicit their agreement: *Of course, Bob was wrong; he was definitely unloving, and not being a good husband.* This "support" only generated more resentment, and Bob responded by resenting her in return. They were playing the victim/perpetrator game, switching roles over and over. Eventually, Jane began an internet relationship with another man; she felt he listened to her. He became her rescuer.

Bob and Jane blamed each other for their feelings rather than seeing that their beliefs were in and from themselves. When they each began to confess their bitterness and harmful actions, they began the journey toward freedom. Bob was also involved in a similar triangle with his ex-wife and daughter, and Jane became involved in this triangle also.

What can we do if the other person isn't willing to see her part? It's irrelevant. As we change and drop our bitterness, we can learn to respond in new ways. All we can do is ask the Lord to show us these areas in our hearts, then respond in confession. He will change us. "Ask and it will be given to you." He will help us see our planks, and change us from swine and dogs into children of the living God, dependent on His power. We cannot change on our own strength. We will continue to be trapped until the Holy Spirit Himself changes us.

**TRANSFORMED
PERSONAL RESPONSIBILITY**

REPENTANCE   FORGIVENESS

GOD

WEAPONS OF RIGHTEOUSNESS

GOD OUR COMFORTER   PERPETRATOR
AND DELIVERER

Begin to look for the ways this triangle plays out in your relationships. The scenarios are endless: a parent who pressures his child to get straight A's, in hopes of rescuing himself from the guilt of being a bad parent; a friend who wants you to align with him against another friend; a child who feels unloved and blames her mother, applying subtle pressure for validation even into adulthood; a husband who demands sex to feel good about himself; a mother who confides in her children about marital issues to gain their support; family members who protect the molester rather than the molested child; a father who takes sides with his son against his new wife; a coworker who sees an employee being abused by the supervisor, but is unwilling to speak up. There are as many examples as there are people.

Take some time and ask the Lord to show you the *planks* in your eye, and how you fit into the victim triangle. You'll be glad you did.

CHAPTER THIRTEEN

The Narrow Gate

Enter by the narrow gate; for the gate is wide and the way is broad that leads to destruction, and many are those who enter by it. For the gate is small and the way is narrow that leads to life, and few are those who find it. (MATTHEW 7:13-14)

God has given us a plan for healing—His roadmap to freedom from deception and sin. Freedom is His ultimate purpose for us, as we described in Chapter Two, *The Big Picture*. We've explained how God wants to transform us by renewing our minds (Romans 12:2). Paul also tells us, "For the mind set on the flesh is death, but the mind set on the spirit is life and peace" (Romans 8:16). So, we have a gate to open, and a path to walk down. God opened the narrow gate for us through the life, death, and resurrection of Christ. Beyond the gate is a path. He is the gate through which we enter, *and* the path we must follow.

Christ is the narrow gate

We've seen that we're justified by Christ. but now must be healed (*sozo*) daily. Even as believers filled with the Holy Spirit, our minds can remain trapped in the habits of self-effort. But God's mercies are new every morning (Lamentations 3:22). He helps us leave behind our fallen ways and embrace life in Him.

Unfortunately, many Christians continue to use *weapons of unrighteousness* to deal with their pain. These powerful negative forces take on a life of their own and prevent us from changing. We must face the fact that we have unrighteousness in our flesh and need to be transformed.

Let's look at God's scriptural plan for healing.

LISTENING TO OURSELVES

"And I say to you that every careless word that men shall speak, they shall render account for it in the day of judgment. For by your words you shall be justified, and by your words you shall be condemned" (Matthew 12:36-37).

Just before uttering these words, Jesus said, "The mouth speaks out of that which fills the heart" (Matthew 12:34). How many of us have really pondered the importance of this statement? Every word we speak reveals our hearts—what we truly believe. By listening to the words that come out of our mouths, we learn what we believe in our minds.

We may not like what we hear, and may even try to deny it. But the evidence of our words is undeniable. This is God's way of showing us the issues in our hearts. Once we hear, we can act.

This is why it's so important that we talk with each other. We need people who will hear us and offer feedback. Jesus said, "What proceeds out of the mouth, this defiles the man" (Matthew 15:11). Listening to our own words, we can begin to identify where the enemy of our souls has deceived us, poisoning and defiling our lives.

EXAMINING OUR ACTIONS

How do we behave toward others? This is another indicator of what is in our hearts. Proverbs tells us, "There is a way which seems right to a man, but its end is the way of death" (Proverbs 14;12). All of us believe our actions are justified. But we can't all be right all of the time! In truth, our deeds reveal what we believe about ourselves and others. Sin tells us that there's something wrong inside us; that our beliefs are inconsistent with scripture. Jesus bore the penalty for our sin, so we're no longer condemned for it. Now, it serves to point out the deception in our lives. When we sin,, we can ask God to show us where we've been deceived. When He does, we can receive the truth.

LOOKING IN THE MIRROR

In the remarkable verse we mentioned earlier, Jesus tells us that we will be judged the way we judge others (Matthew 7:1-2). We can easily miss the significance of this scripture, especially in the context of healing. We could infer that our judgment of others is a clear indication of *what is inside of us*. Judging involves seeing and drawing conclusions. Christ is referring to the way we see others—which is a mirror reflection of how we see ourselves. If we look at the behavior of others and conclude they don't love us, it may indicate that we have believed a lie: *I'm not loved*. And, we'll project our feelings onto the other person. We feel that we're not good enough, so we'll judge the other person as not good enough. Psychology refers to this as *projection,* but God simply calls it *judgment*. The faults we see in others are inside of us.

FINDING THE BEAMS

"Why do you look at the speck that is in your brother's eye, but do not notice the log that is in your own eye? Or how can you say to your brother, 'Let me take the speck out of your eye,' and behold, the log is in your own eye? You hypocrite, first take the log out of your own eye, and then you will see clearly to take the speck out of your brother's eye" (Matthew 7:3-5).

What's interesting about this scripture is that the thing in our eyes (the plank or beam) is significantly larger than what's our neighbor's eye (the speck). Our perceptions are warped by our experiences. They are corrupted by sin and deception. We can't perceive life any other way until God changes us.

As we've discussed, these beams support the structure of our minds—the things we think, feel and believe. Scripture refers to each of us as God's temple ((1 Corinthians 6:19). He is ripping out the structures (beams) of our minds so He can replace them with something new—the truth. Jesus Himself is now our foundation. We must cooperate in this process by asking Him to show us those planks.

"Do not give what is holy to the dogs, and do not throw your pearls before swine, lest they trample them under their feet, and turn and tear you to pieces" (Matthew 7:56).

Unfortunately, some people are unwilling to look at the truth. They prefer to blame others for their feelings. In my experience it is fruitless to try to help those who won't take responsibility for their own sin. As we've said, God has a path for us, and it involves confessing, forgiving, taking responsibility. If we're unwilling to walk down that path, we miss God's will.

We must take responsibility for our own feelings and find the planks in our eyes. But how can we do that if we can't identify them on our own?

"Ask and it shall be given, seek and you will find, knock and it shall be open to you" (Matthew 7:7).

We pray, *"Lord, show me my planks!"* It's that simple. We ask, he responds. And this is one prayer that He can count on Him answering positively.

TAKING OUR THOUGHTS CAPTIVE

As we pay attention to our thoughts and words to uncover our false beliefs, we must then learn how to deal scripturally with them. Paul speaks of "taking every thought captive" (2 Corinthians 10:5). This is a key scripture in God's blueprint for healing, because it tells us how to deal with the deception, pain and sin we discover in our minds and hearts. Just as we must pay attention to what we say, Paul tells us to take note of every thought.

This is harder than it sounds. In my experience, most of us reject what we think. Why? Because our thoughts cause us pain and suffering. So, we simply deny their existence.

After years of practice at denying and ignoring our thoughts, we must be taught a different way. It is Christ's Spirit dwelling in us that allows us to hear. We have the mind of Christ (1 Corinthians 2:16), and instead of running from these painful thoughts, we can take them captive to Christ, asking Him to reveal our hearts. The next part is crucial: We must listen intently. We might be inclined to simply reject our thoughts as being sinful, but that misses the point. These thoughts are really God showing us the areas He wants to heal and transform. We must bring them to Him, not try to push them out of our minds.

> We must take every thought captive to Christ, and cast down every lofty thing that exalts itself against Christ.

As we've learned, "obedience" means to *listen attentively*. Obeying in this situation is not rushing out to do something, but rather simply listening to what God has to say. What are my thoughts telling me? When people reach this point, after confessing their sin and demolishing their strongholds, the change can be dramatic. The truth sparks a reaction that changes the way they think and feel. Just as Jesus spoke the world into existence, He speaks into our hearts. The result is a miracle, where the truth is implanted and we're set free.

TEARING DOWN STRONGHOLDS

The word translated "stronghold" or "fortress" in the Bible was also used in New Testament times to denote a prison. Contrary to popular belief, a stronghold is not an external thing that we can pull down simply by praying against it. Strongholds are very personal. They are internal things that live in our very own minds. When we believe lies, we allow Satan to establish a prison of deception in us. Believing a lie is dangerous; our eternal destiny depends on us believing the truth. The urgency of this issue begins to become apparent.

To experience healing, we must understand strongholds and learn how to tear them down. That means confessing our sin and deception, and hearing the Truth of God. Faith comes by hearing, and hearing by the Word of God—Jesus (Romans 10: 17). Without biblical faith we cannot be saved. And the same applies to our day-to-day transformation.

CASTING DOWN VAIN IMAGINATIONS

A vain imagination or *speculation* is anything we embrace that is inconsistent with God's scriptural plan. Some examples:

I should have done this...
I could have done that...
If only this would happen...
I wish this had happened...
I wish I had been this...
I can figure this out on my own...
I shouldn't feel this way...
I should be able to deal with this...

These illustrate how we try to deal with pain out of our own experience, rather than going to God for truth. This is fruitless because the original problem is that we are deceived. We can't find the truth in our own brains, because it's not there! This effort is really a subtle form of self-exaltation, part of a long tradition. Scripture tells us that Satan exalted himself above God; Adam and Eve did too, when they chose to believe the lie. Cain did the same thing when he brought an unacceptable sacrifice to God. And we exalt ourselves above God when we disobey Him, depending on our own strength, minds, and knowledge.

EVERY LOFTY THING

Along with vain imaginations or speculations, we're told to destroy "every lofty thing raised up against the knowledge of God." What might this include? Here are some candidates:

- Sinful means used to accomplish our desires
- Worldly wisdom that seems right but leads to spiritual death.
- Actions that exalt us over others.

CONFESSING

When we confess our sin, Christ removes it through His atoning sacrifice. Then, as we continue to confess, He cleanses us (1 John 1:9) and replaces deception with truth. Confessing our sin allows the Holy Spirit to work in us. This contrasts with our natural tendency to hide, rationalize, intellectualize, and try to work things out in our own minds. God tells us to listen to Him, not figure things out on our own. After all, our minds are what got us into the mess we're in. That's why the Word of God is so beneficial—it exists outside our own experience. And we need to hear His voice, speaking to us from outside ourselves. We also need each other. Other believers can show us the truth and lead us to a new experience.

PUTTING ON THE MIND OF CHRIST

We seek healing to find relief from our pain—emotional and physical. When our minds accept negative self-concepts, the brain creates chemicals that cause painful feelings in our bodies. Thus, feeling unloved leads to a chemical change in the body that we experience as anxiety, fear, stress, tension, etc. We've noted the profound insight expressed by the proverb, "...As he thinks within himself, so he is" (Proverbs 23:7). An equivalent in modern psychology is cognitive theory, which holds that what a man believes leads to an emotional feeling. How we view an event will determine whether we feel pain or joy.

Cognitive psychology teaches people to rewrite their perceptions of events. As Christians, we can do this by allowing God to tell us the truth about our lives. Our minds only know what they've experienced. As a computer is bound by its programming, we're bound by our experience. If the mind believes it is unloved, it can never free itself from this belief. An unregenerate man needs the truth, but that truth lies outside of his experience. The truth is a person—Jesus Christ. He gives us information beyond our direct experience, speaking not only to our hearts, but to our minds and souls. Regarding the Holy Spirit, Jesus said, "He will teach you all things...(John 14:26), and "He shall take of mine, and shall disclose it to you" (John 16:15).

The mind is a place of instability. As James said, "A double minded man is unstable in all his ways" (James 1:8). When we know in our hearts that God loves, but our minds believe that we're unloved or unlovable, this is fertile ground for instability, pain and sin. Without Christ, people must rely on their intellectual resources to calm this inner turmoil. But a deceived mind cannot discover the truth, much less tell it! Christians have the transforming power of Jesus, the truth, which wipes away the program of the old lie. God speaks peace to those places of turmoil. The conflict between mind and heart ceases.

Believers with God's image restored can hear what they were unable to before. A man who suffered abuse as a child may never have heard a kind, loving word. He may have grown up without God's love, ignorant of His ways. Now an adult, He desperately needs God's approval. He needs to hear that in his heavenly Father's eyes, he is good. Through God's Spirit, he can hear that wonderful truth. God can then teach him what he never knew—how to forgive. The voice of God redeems his past and destroys the power of sin over him. This is putting on the mind of Christ. This is the kingdom of God invading the dark stronghold where deception reigned. And it's available to every Christian. Jesus, the Alpha and Omega, wants to redeem every corner of our lives—past, present and future. Through the gift of confession, the past can be undone. We can reclaim what the enemy has stolen

TAKING THE YOKE

God made it so simple! Jesus said, "Come to Me, all who are weary and heavy laden, and I will give you rest. Take My yoke upon you, and learn from Me, for I am gentle and humble in heart; and you shall find rest for your souls. For my yoke is easy and my load is light" (Matthew 11:28-30). This is in contrast to the Pharisees, who according to Jesus placed yokes on people they were unable to lift themselves.

We make things so difficult! We impose rules and regulations on ourselves, and conjure up images of what a mature Christian should be like. The problem is, we don't know what wholeness looks like because we haven't experienced it. None of us has yet been fully transformed.

Jesus said, "You are to be perfect, as your heavenly Father is perfect" (Matthew 5:48). The word "perfect" in this context means *mature-minded*. As we grow in Christ, our He renews our minds through the truth, leading to His model of perfection. With each new day, our minds are less bound by darkness, with fewer false beliefs. And He reveals the areas that are not yet perfect.

On this path of renewal, God gives us a simple scriptural plan for healing. We don't overcome deception by our own power, ability, righteousness, cunning or craftiness. We do it through the power of the Holy Spirit living in us.

Simple.

But simple does not mean easy or pain-free. As Christ overcame the world through suffering, we too must overcome our sinful nature through suffering. We discovered in Chapter Five *(Pain is a Good Thing)* that pain has a purpose.

Once we accept suffering as part of the package, we find that the way forward is simple indeed: God shows us our false beliefs. We agree with Him—we confess. And He cleanses us.

This is the easy yoke that Jesus spoke of—the light burden. Christ takes our burden and places it on His own shoulders. Then He heals us, completely.

That is the small gate, and the narrow path.

CHAPTER FOURTEEN

Confession

Therefore confess your sins to each other and pray for each other so that you may be healed. The prayer of a righteous man is powerful and effective. (JAMES 5:16)

God has a plan and purpose for His people, but as history shows, we're apt to do things every way but His. Like Adam and Eve, we seek knowledge instead of relationship. It should be clear that we don't need more knowledge! In fact, God has made the way to wholeness perfectly simple—so simple that "wise" men can't comprehend it. As Jesus said, "I thank thee, O Father, Lord of heaven and earth, that thou hast hid these things from the wise and prudent, and hast revealed them unto babes; even so, Father; for so it seemed good in thy sight" (Mathew 11:25). What has God hidden? The things of the Kingdom.

After Adam and Eve sinned, they hid from God. But of course, He found them. God tells us this story to let us know that we can't hide from Him. As with those first humans, He knows exactly where we are! He sees us, naked and ashamed, hiding in our sin. Of course, Adam and Eve could have approached God on their own and confessed their sin. They didn't. Even more intriguing, before they ate that forbidden fruit they could have come to Him and confessed the lie they had believed. But it caused them such pain that in their deception they sinned. And then, they hid from their maker.

We do the very same thing.

We must confess our sin to God—first, that we've been hiding just like Adam and Eve. Then, that we're unable to approach Him on our own. In this we're simply agreeing with God, which is what *confession* really means. Then, God helps us walk out of the darkness into the light—just as He did with that first pair.

When we confess our sin, we're finally able to see the truth: Our sin is no longer counted against us. In Christ, *there is no condemnation*. He doesn't even remember it. Then, He cleanses us. And He shows us that our sin is actually a *tool* He can use to heal us. In Christ, even our sin has a purpose: showing us the deception we've embraced in our natural minds. When He brings the light of truth into those areas, we're set free. No longer will those lies cause us pain. No longer will we use sin to take that pain away. And that's transformation!

But God cannot do any of this until we confess our sin. James gives us some straightforward instruction: *"confess your sins to each other and pray for each other so that you may be healed"* (James 5:16). If we want to be healed, we must follow this direction. We must know the truth of confession. And the truth will set us free.

Agreeing with God means that if He calls something sin, we do too. In this, the flesh will always rise up against the spirit. Our natural impulse is always to cover up our sin. The Holy Spirit will lead us to confess it, agreeing with God and opening ourselves up to others. In confessing, we crucify the flesh. Hiding our sin is the work of unrighteousness. Confessing it is the work of righteousness.

Confession has a much greater purpose than achieving our forgiveness. It's the key that unlocks the power of God to renew our minds, heal us, and change us into Christ's image. Three simple words unlock this narrow gate: *Father, forgive me!* With these words we find forgiveness, but also something more, something wondrous and miraculous: God changes us. He begins to remove the filth from our lives. He cleanses us of our unrighteousness. Confession is a powerful thing. It achieves what we can't do on our own. It overcomes our sin and deception. Without it there is no healing, no transformation.

EIGHT TRUTHS OF CONFESSION:

1. Confession is the prayer of the righteous.

In the passage that opens this chapter, James urges us to confess our sins to each other and pray for each other so that we may be healed. Then in the same verse, he says, "The effective prayer of a righteous man can accomplish much." What would the *prayer of a righteous man* consist of? The things he just mentioned! *Confession* is part of the prayer of the righteous. It's how a righteous person talks to the Lord. Are you confessing something you're ashamed of? Take heart; the Bible says you're doing something righteous.

The righteous man confesses his sin. How often? As many times as it appears. The righteous man knows that the Lord has promised to heal him through his confession. So he continues to confess, and waits upon the Lord. The righteous man confesses not just to God, but to his fellow believers, without fearing what they might think of him. He lives to please God, not other people. He knows that the Father is pleased by the blood of Christ, and that alone assures his acceptance.

2. Confession has a purpose.

We don't confess merely to humiliate ourselves. The goal is nothing less than our transformation into the image of Christ. When we confess, he forgives, cleanses, heals and renews us. We can't do this work in ourselves. Only Christ can transform us. But He does it through the power of our confession.

3. Confession leads to repentance.

When we hear the confession of sin come out of our own mouths, it leads us naturally to repent. Three simple words: *Father, forgive me.*

4. Confession is powerful.

When we confess our sins to each other, something very powerful takes place in the spiritual realm. We unlock the power of God to heal us, and the enemy quickly begins to lose ground. We begin to tear down strongholds, dismantling the very obstacles that have prevented us from hearing God's truth.

5. *Confession brings healing.*

God wants us to confess so He can heal us. There is no other way for us to experience His transforming power. He wants us to be free from the deception in our minds. He wants us to trust Him. He wants us to have fellowship with Him and with one another.

6. *Confession is the first step to renewing our minds.*

When Christ reveals Truth to our deception, we are set free. Our mind is renewed. We no longer sin to deal with the pain of the lie.

7. *Confession is our greatest weapon.*

When Satan lies to us, our first instinct is to try to rid ourselves of the pain of the lie, as Adam and Eve did. But the power of confession is greater than our flesh. Rather than fighting the enemy in our own strength, we simply come to God and confess our sin. We agree quickly with our accuser, as Jesus advised, tell the Lord what we've been believing: *Lord, I have believed the lie that I'm not good enough. I have believed the lie that I'm not loved. Lord, show me the Truth.*

8. *Confession equals transformation.*

Confession is the outward expression of inner transformation. As Jesus said, we speak out of the abundance of our hearts. When we confess, we make a conscious choice to expose our hearts, and the fruit is transformation. They go hand in hand.

The consequence of sin is more sin. If we believe we can stop it on our own, we deceive ourselves. It is impossible to stop sinning out of self-effort. Sin is more powerful than our flesh. But Christ in us, who has power over sin, cleanses us of our unrighteousness when we confess and admit our faults (1 John 1:9).

This first aspect of sin is what we have done. Our unforgiveness, vows, judgment, and majority of our sins, are acted upon to protect us from the physical and emotional pain caused by the lies that we believed throughout our lives.

Confession

THE POWER OF CONFESSION

People usually come to my office because they're in pain—grappling with addictions, affairs, anger, and other sinful behavior. They've reached the end of their rope, and are desperate for freedom. And these are Christian clients! Most have been through healing seminars, weekend retreats, and other church-related programs. Although the stories vary, one common feature is always present: They've all been taught that they *can overcome their sinful behavior*. The vehicle might be Bible study, accountability groups, discipleship programs, or just sheer willpower, but they can do it!

How sad and unnecessary.

Brian was a 24 year-old married man involved in pornography. He had learned this behavior at the age of 12. He used it compulsively to make himself feel good. The programs he had been through taught him to accept that he had a problem. He was taught to read his bible daily, join an accountability group, and avoid looking at women. But he was still in the powerful grip of this addiction. He felt like a failure. He had confessed his sin, and knew that God had forgiven him. But he couldn't stop.

> Confession of sinful behavior is the first step.

Brian's attempts to stop his sinful behavior were like pruning a bush. The bush is invigorated by the pruning, and comes back stronger! The apostle Paul describes this as the power of sin within us: The things we don't want to do, we do. When we try to conquer sinful behavior through self-will and determination, we set ourselves up for failure. This is a spiritual fact. Sin can never be overcome by trying. But unfortunately, this message of self-reliance has become the gospel of this age.

Sin can only be removed by the blood of Jesus Christ. Paul states, "We have this treasure (Christ) in earthen vessels so that we know that it is not of our own power, but God's power." Scripture gives a clear directive on how God will manifest His power in us: If we confess our sin, He is faithful to forgive us, and the blood of Jesus Christ cleanses us of all unrighteousness.

Brian and I prayed together, asking God to show Him *why* he was engaged in pornography. Part of Brian's confession was to admit what he was really feeling—the pain that he was trying to dull with this fruitless activity. This honesty is just as important as asking for forgiveness. Unless we admit what is in us, how can we hear what the Lord is trying to change?

We started to delve into those feelings together. Brian pointed the finger at his wife: she never validated him, and made him feel inadequate. He wasn't good enough. So of course, he took refuge in pornography. That took away his pain—for awhile. None of the women he viewed ever made him feel he was "not good enough."

> Through the act of confession, we hear the lie.

Through Brian's confession, we heard the lie: "I'm not good enough." This simple lie was the source of his pain. The sinful behavior was his means of trying to overcome this deception and make himself feel like he *was* good enough. Of course, this feeling of inadequacy originated early in his childhood. His parents, just like his wife, never validated him. In fact, they hit him repeatedly for his mistakes, and often wouldn't tell him why he was being disciplined. Brian vowed never to treat his own children that way, and never to be like his parents.

During this time, his older brother introduced him to pornography. It made him feel good. He would gaze at these beautiful women and imagine that they loved him. In this fantasy world, he *was* good enough.

I asked Brian if he had any resentment towards his parents for the way they treated him. He told me quickly, "I've already taken care of that. I've already forgiven them." Brian had been through church programs, accountability groups, and weekend retreats for addictions. He had been taught to forgive those who hurt him. But for some reason, he was still in pain. I pressed a little further. "I don't need to look at the past," he insisted. He had been taught in church to "forget what lies behind." He was sure his sinful behavior and painful feelings were about the present, not the past.

> Confession reveals our resentment, vows, and judgment.

Then I asked him something different: Had he ever asked God to forgive him for resenting his parents? We asked God to search his heart, and He soon revealed several incidents where Brian had indeed harbored resentment. As Brian confessed his resentment and vows of self-protection, the power of sin dissipated. He came to realize that this sin was a powerful enticement of the enemy to not trust in God for His strength. And he discovered the wonderful truth that there was now no more condemnation for sin. His sinful patterns simply exposed his fruitless ways of dealing with his pain. He began to seek God for comfort, rather than turning to sex, pornography or anger.

This type of healing can only be accomplished through confession. But many church environments don't foster confession as a lifestyle. Even therapists may ignore its importance, focusing instead on insights gained through delving into personal history. For Christians who lack this confessional environment, I encourage them seek it out. God's people are being ravaged by sin and deception of all sorts. Only confessing our sin will remove this virus. I believe that all Christian leaders, therapists, friends, brothers, and sisters, must become adept at assisting one another in the process of confession.

TAKING THE FIRST STEP

Starting the practice of confession can be difficult since we're so steeped in self-effort. Confession is the way of the Spirit, and not the flesh. Many of us still fear that we'll be condemned for our sin. We're hiding like Adam and Eve, naked and ashamed. We must trust that when we confess what we've been hiding, God will be there to clothe us.

WALKING ON

Transformation occurs as we crucify our flesh through confession. In Christ we are no longer in sin, but it still has power in our flesh. When a past sin remains unconfessed, it continues to wreak destruction in our temporal lives. Why else would we be admonished to examine ourselves and take up our cross daily? We must confess each sin the Holy Spirit reveals. Most of us are rampant with unconfessed sin, resentment, judgments and vows. We have accepted the lie that a one-time confession of Jesus as Lord takes care of everything. But it does not.

It's important to realize that confession is about our old nature, not who we really are in Christ. Confession can become a lifestyle. It is, in fact, the lifestyle of the righteous—which all of us are as believers.

CHAPTER FIFTEEN

Receiving the Truth

Grace and truth were realized through Jesus Christ. (JOHN 1:17)

The Spirit searches all things, even the deep things of God. For who among men knows the thoughts of a man except the man's spirit within him? In the same way no one knows the thoughts of God except the Spirit of God. We have not received the spirit of the world but the Spirit who is from God, that we may understand what God has freely given us. This is what we speak, not in words taught us by human wisdom but in words taught by the Spirit, expressing spiritual truths in spiritual words. The man without the Spirit does not accept the things that come from the Spirit of God, for they are foolishness to him, and he cannot understand them, because they are spiritually discerned. The spiritual man makes judgments about all things, but he himself is not subject to any man's judgment: 'For who has known the mind of the Lord that he may instruct him?' But we have the mind of Christ.

(1 CORINTHIANS 2:10-16)

The journey we've described in the previous chapters always begins with pain. That's what makes us realize something is wrong, and seek healing. We've explained the process of exposing our hearts to God, listening to our thoughts and words, allowing Him to reveal our lies and strongholds. We've learned to put down our weapons of protection, break our vows and confess our sin.

What's left? In Ephesians, Paul says Christ gave Himself for his church, "...that He might sanctify her, having cleansed her by the washing of water with the word..." (Ephesians 5:26). The areas that were once polluted with lies must now be cleansed and filled with God's word. He demonstrated this cleansing when He washed the disciples' feet. In that case, the Word of God in human flesh washed them literally and physically. Now, He does the same for us in the spirit.

Jesus is not just our source for truth; He is truth itself. He is "the Alpha and the Omega, the first and the last, the beginning and the end" (Revelation 22:12), and of course He is "the way, the truth and the life" (John 14:6). The wondrous thing about truth is that it sets us free.

So how do we receive the freeing truth that is Christ? Let's look a little closer.

> Telling ourselves truth is not the same as hearing it from God

First, we must realize a harsh fact: Unregenerate people do not have access to the truth of Christ. As the scripture that opens this chapter makes clear, the natural man cannot receive the things of the Spirit of God. Unbelievers can only depend on their human wisdom, which is foolishness to God. They seek to heal themselves through insight and psychological principles. As the saying goes, they're rearranging the deck chairs on the Titanic.

For Christians, on the other hand, the ship has already sunk, and been raised back up from the depths! Now God is working in us the resurrection power of Christ. His truth destroys the deception that keeps us depending on our old nature. We can now live in our new nature. So, why would we seek help from those who don't know this truth?

Telling ourselves the truth is not the same as hearing it from God. Our intellects cannot give us the truth we need. The world tells us that truth is accessible to all. That may be so regarding certain temporal truth, but not spiritual truth. If Jesus Himself is the truth, we can only know truth by knowing Him. And communing with other believers is part of that: As He said, where two or more are gathered in His name, Christ is there in our midst.

HEARING THE TRUTH FROM GOD

My sheep hear my voice, and I know them, and they follow me: And I give unto them eternal life; and they shall never perish, neither shall any man pluck them out of my hand. (John 10:27-28)

The scriptures tell us to "put on the mind of Christ." This is how we come to understand what God has freely given us. God heals us by revealing the truth to our hearts. We've said this in many ways throughout this book, because it's so important! Unfortunately, many Christians are still bound by their own intellects in their search for truth.

So, how does all this fit in the healing process we've described?

Once our self- protective mechanisms of sin, vows and judgment are torn down, all that is left is the lie—that false belief at the core of our being that causes our pain. This is where it's critical to bring every thought captive to Christ, as Paul says. When I reach this point with clients, I simply ask God to tell them the truth. In this, we are depending on the very promise of God that we will *hear His voice*.

This raises an interesting question: How do we hear God? In these counseling situations, we trust God to speak His truth directly to the person's mind and heart. And it happens: They hear the words in their minds. There is a *knowing* that He speaks to them. It's as if they're simply thinking, and the thought passes through their minds.

Does this sound strange or even dangerous? Let's consider: What, after all, does it mean to *put on the mind of Christ*? Is it not taking every thought captive to Him, and then listening to what He has to say? Some would call this revelation, which it certainly is. But in many religious circles, we've made the concept of hearing God too complicated.

If Jesus lives in us, where does *us* end and Christ begin? We understand that we are not God, and our flesh is sinful. But He did say "I have called you friends, for all things that I have heard from my Father I have made known to you" (John 15: 15). We also have this assurance from James: "If any man lacks wisdom, let him ask of God, who gives to all men generously and without reproach, and it will be given to him" (James 1:5). How will we receive that wisdom? How will God reveal Himself to us? Can it not be something so simple as capturing our own thought—the thought He places in us? Certainly, it can. How does this work out in real life? We simply ask God to tell us the truth. In my counseling, I've rarely encountered anyone who, upon asking, could not hear the voice of God in their inner being.

My experience with Jim provides a good example. Like so many troubled people, Jim's problems stemmed from a history of abuse—in his case, at the hands of his mother. As we joined together in prayer, I spoke up first: "God, Jim believes he's not *good enough*. Would you tell him the truth? Take him back, Lord, to the place where his mother was abusing him, telling him he was bad, blaming him for her anger. And tell him how you see those things."

By now, Jim had been through considerable counseling and learned to listen for God's voice. Seemingly out of nowhere, he had a thought: *It was my mother's issue—not mine!* He knew that this was Christ. How did he know? Because God spoke something that Jim alone could receive. Had I told him the same thing, he may have recognized it intellectually as *a truth*. But when God says it, it becomes *The Truth*—personalized just for Jim. God alone can search the deep places of our hearts; He knows the perfect word to speak.

Jim had suffered with a lie all his life. God's revelation freed him: *It was your mother's issue that caused her to abuse you.* It wasn't that he wasn't good enough. It wasn't about him at all.

I'm constantly amazed to hear what God speaks to his children—things we could never imagine if we tried. He knows our hearts, and what words will set us free. But what about the written word of God? Are we substituting our subjective thoughts for the truth of scripture? Actually, God often speaks to our minds *through* the scriptures. He'll bring to mind a passage we've read, one that meant something to us earlier. And often, it will be just the truth we need to break the power of the lie.

Pat had endured molestation from her father as a child. As a result, she struggled with the lie that she was *dirty*. As we prayed and talked, scriptures began floating into her mind: "I know the plans I have for you for;

Receiving the Truth

plans for good and not evil." "You meant evil against me, but God meant it for good." "Though your sins be as scarlet, they shall be white as snow." This last scripture had a special significance for Pat. Often, God uses scripture to convey His truth. And sometimes He simply speaks truth in words we can understand.

But isn't reading scripture enough? It could be, if we know the specific truth God wants to speak to us in a given moment. The psalms speak of hiding God's word in our hearts. When we do that, He brings scriptures to our remembrance as we deal with specific issues. But reading scripture without God's leading is like using a shotgun to shoot a duck—blindfolded. We may hit the duck, and we may not. By asking God to give us the truth for a specific lie, we become like expert marksmen with high powered telescopes, zeroing in on our target. Military marksmen, properly trained and equipped, can hit a small object from several hundred yards away. Their lives and the lives of others depend on their accuracy. Our lives in Christ also depend on our accuracy in handling God's word.

I often hear people say, "Other people hear from God; not me." But the beauty of our relationship with Christ is that all of us can hear from Him, great or small. One of my greatest joys is working with children and teens who have learned to hear the Lord's voice. We can train our children in the ways of God. We typically think this means imposing systems of behavior or rules. As we should know, these are doomed to fail. But we can teach them to confess their sin, to forgive, to listen to God. Unlike their elders, these children, with relatively little experience in sin and deception, are able to grab hold of God in a very effective and innocent way.

As I write this, my little daughter is eight years old. When other children hurt her, she feels resentment like any child would. But in these moments, I've been gratified to hear her ask Christ to forgive her for resenting them. God speaks truth that is utterly personal to her—things her mother and I never could have imagined—and she has learned to hear Him. He knows her better than we do. We've also learned to trust the voice of God in our daughter, the same way I trust Him to speak to every one of my clients.

Another person who learned to hear God's voice was Donnie, who came to me expressing that he felt "unloved." Together we asked God to show him where this belief originated. His sense was overwhelming that "It's always been there." This was odd, since he came from a very nice, loving family; it even confused him. But behind the nice exterior was a disturbing truth: Donnie was adopted; his biological mother had abandoned him at birth. And he knew this.

Donnie felt a deep hatred and resentment for this woman who had rejected and abandoned him. He also hated and resented himself, and felt it must all have been his fault somehow. As we prayed, he confessed his feelings and repented. Then God addressed the specific lie that haunted him: He was unloved.

The thought passed through Donnie's mind: "I have *always* been loved. God Himself loves me!" At this point, he had the same question that many people would: How can I know that this is God speaking to me? Couldn't it just be my own mind?

Good question. I asked him, "Well, what has your mind been telling you up till now?"

"That no one loves me."

"Then why now would you believe that this is from your own mind"

Donnie had been listening to a lie all his life. But this day, he heard a different truth.

God makes it easy for us to hear Him! We are His sheep, and as He said, we know His voice. It's not hard or complicated. God is only too willing to tell us the truth, if we ask. In Philippians, Paul describes his attitude of continual striving for the truth, saying, "Let us therefore, as many as are perfect, have this attitude; and if in anything you have a different attitude, God will reveal that also to you" God watches over His word to perform it, so if He says will hear His voice—we will.

I once spoke to a Christian leader who expressed his fear that if we stress this kind of personal guidance, people would take advantage of God's grace. They would excuse their sin and claim that God was guiding them. Any of us who've been around Christians much know that this can indeed happen. When it does, we must try to help the misguided ones see their sin. I've heard Christians justify sexual sin, saying, "God knows we love each other. He's OK with it." Or, they justify divorce with, "God told me it's OK." I feel a responsibility to confront these people in love, but when they don't respond I trust God to convict them. Then, I continue to love.

I know that there is now no condemnation for sin. Jesus is continually taking their sin, even while they are in it. They're simply deceived. But the Lord in them is always greater than the deception. I continue to believe He's working in them, even if I can't see the fruit.

But if they continue in sin, doesn't that mean they aren't really Christians? Maybe. But even in that case, Paul instructs us to not judge. That job belongs to the Holy Spirit. He wants *us* to love—even our enemies. My policy is to believe everybody until the Lord instructs me otherwise.

When Anna's husband had an affair, she was filled with pain. She felt betrayed, but more than that, she felt used. I learned that Anna was the main breadwinner in the home, which certainly contributed to her feelings. She had also developed a strong disdain for her husband, which showed in her words and behavior. Their relationship deteriorated and he eventually strayed.

Anna knew she had scriptural grounds for divorce. But God began to stir something in her. He showed her the contempt she had allowed into her heart and how it caused her to push her husband away. She had sinned too, and her sin was no better than his in God's eyes. Her attitude began to change. God told her to forgive her husband. Forgiveness can overcome even a spouse's adultery. And refusing to forgive is just as great a sin.

Many Christians would have counseled Anna to leave her marriage. She certainly had the right. But God Himself is our example: He didn't give up on His people even when they were "adulterous," worshipping idols. And we all are like the adulterous Israelites in some ways. But the blood of Jesus is greater than any sin.

In Anna's case, God's voice superceded the prevalent beliefs around her. And His conviction trumped human understanding. She responded, and today she is giving glory to God for restoring her marriage.

My habit when confronting these difficult issues is to ask people "What do you believe the Lord is saying to you?" Of course, sometimes they're so distraught that they simply need guidance. But learning to hear God's voice is the way to freedom.

A FINAL NOTE

It is important that those counseling others have submitted to healing and transformation themselves. How can we help others hear God if we doubt His voice ourselves? This is where the Body of Christ is so important. As we seek to hear God, we find safety in submitting to other believers. Scripture is clear that we are to confess our sins one to another. This community of believers protects us from misusing the grace of God

CHAPTER SIXTEEN

Putting it all Together

Blessed is a man who perseveres under trial; for once he has been approved, he will receive the crown of life which the Lord has promised to those who love Him.
(JAMES 1:12)

The way to transformation is narrow, as Jesus said. We've discussed various aspects of it. Now, let's put it all together.

People who seek help are usually motivated by one of two things: emotional *pain* from a crisis, or a besetting *sin*. Both of these point to something wrong deep in our hearts. But in fact, *all* of us need to be transformed. As John said, "If we say we that we have no sin, we are deceiving ourselves" (1 John 1:8). Here are some practical guidelines from real life that will help as you seek healing—for yourself or someone you care about:

1. CONNECTING THE PAIN TO THE BELIEF

People seeking help usually start where it hurts. They'll describe their pain: *I feel so angry! I'm hurting! How could this have happened?* It's important at this point that they have a counselor, friend or pastor to share their feelings with. And they must then connect their feeling with the *belief* that's causing it.

When someone tells me how much they hurt, I usually ask, "What are you *believing* that makes you feel this way?." This may seem like a strange question, but as they consider and pray about it, God usually reveals a thought:

I'm not loved, or *I'm abandoned*. We continue to ask until a belief surfaces in the person's mind. (You'll find a list of lies or false beliefs in Chapter Six: *Lies We Believe*.) It's important to understand that our pain does not come from the event, but rather from what we *believe* about the event.

We must also enlist the aid of the Holy Spirit through simple prayer, such as, "Lord, would you show us the belief that is producing this feeling?" During this process, several beliefs may surface. This is normal; I call it *dumping*. As a therapist, I simply write down the beliefs and keep a record of each one. And I explain that these intense feelings may come from several lies being triggered at once: *I'm unloved. I'm alone. I'm used. I'm dirty.* This is why we must take *every* thought captive to Jesus—one lie at a time. One reason we often feel overwhelmed is that we try to make all our feelings go away at once. And we can't handle it. But when we tackle issues individually, God brings clarity to each one and gives us hope to continue the process.

It's also important to be patient. Most of us aren't used to looking for our hidden beliefs. We try to deal with emotions through our intellect. We must learn to listen and accept what comes into our minds and hearts, believing that as we ask, God will answer. Few of us were trained as children to hear the voice of God. We may have learned to memorize scripture, study, or do other good things—but not to listen to the Holy Spirit. This is very important.

2. ADDRESSING THE STRONGHOLD

Once we recognize the false beliefs in our minds, we address them one at a time. When Sally tells me she feels unloved by a friend, we take that specific thought captive to the obedience (attentive listening) of Christ. I pray, "Lord, would you show Sally where she first believed this lie that she is unloved?" Then—like a ball in water—a thought, memory or word will pop up.

I tell Sally, "Don't try to censor your thoughts." This censoring and analyzing is what we do throughout our lives to limit the pain associated with an event or belief. Instead, we just want to hear what God is pointing out to us. We are not searching; He is searching us. With patience and quiet, the memory will eventually come to mind. Other information can emerge too. We ask God what this information means, and keep listening. We ask God to show the person any resentment in this memory towards anyone. It could be towards others, self or God. And it's important to recognize that when we believe a lie that we're *unloved*, for example, there may be plenty of evidence to support it. The person in question may, in fact, not love us. But if we're holding resentment and unforgiveness in our hearts, we must confess it.

At this point I lead Sally in a prayer of confession: "Lord, forgive me for the resentment I'm holding in my heart towards my friend!" I usually ask God to reveal resentment first and then vows, judgment and sin. But as we speak about our painful memories, those vows and judgments typically surface on their own.

3. ASKING AGAIN AND AGAIN

This is where patience and perseverance are necessary. We are looking for the lie's origin—the incident that first introduced it. I might pray, "Lord, would you show Sally where she first believed the lie that she was unloved?" For each memory that comes up, I ask God to show her any resentment. As she talks, I'm also listening to hear any unconfessed sin, vows or judgments.

We do this over and over, until no more answers come. A bit of instruction is crucial here: We're seeking to hear the voice of the Holy Spirit, not to think. Thinking implies *figuring things out* on our own, without God. This leads us back into the familiar trap of ignoring our memories because of the pain they bring. The process of asking and listening does an end-run around the resistance that most counselors experience. We're simply depending on God to reveal the unconfessed sin in the person's life. Seeking the origin of the lie may take minutes, or hours. My sessions typically last about an hour, but much gets accomplished in that brief time! Locating and resolving a lie can take days, or as little as a few minutes. For people who've developed a habit of denying their emotional pain, healing may take awhile. But we persist, and offer encouragement each step of the way. We ask until no more events surface.. This dialog with God becomes easier the more we engage it. We learn to trust the Holy Spirit within, and as promised, He reveals the things of Christ to us.

4. FINDING FREEDOM IN THE TRUTH

When we finally arrive at the origin of the lie, we ask Jesus to replace it with truth. We've destroyed the stronghold that prevented us from hearing Him.

I ask, "Lord, would you show Sally the truth that you want her to know about her belief that she is unloved?" We trust God to speak the truth to her at that very place where the pain began. We know that His sheep hear His voice, and in my experience, most people do hear God at this point. I've counseled with adults, teens and children as young as three. I'm amazed to hear the truth that God speaks to His children, young and old. It is always very personal. Only God's voice can break a painful belief and replace it with the truth. My voice cannot.

We shouldn't assume we know what someone needs to hear. Most of what I say in therapy is to prepare the client to hear Christ, the source of truth and life. In a sense, we are priests, and our job is to lead the person to Jesus—whose words alone can heal and transform.

5. STARTING OVER

We'd like to believe that we can forgive once, and that will be sufficient. But in fact, a single event can produce many painful beliefs. And as we discuss in Chapter 9: *Resentment*, each one must be dealt with separately. Our minds are temporal and limited. I tell clients that the Lord may bring them back to an event they had previously encountered. This is very normal. When they protest that they've "been here before," I urge them to go there anyway. Remember, we're trusting that God is revealing things as we ask Him. He knows where to go. When we do this, there's very likely something there we need to see.

6. CONFESSING COMPLETELY

I encourage people to be very specific in their confessions: "Lord, forgive me for resenting my wife for the time she struck up an online relationship with another man, and made me feel unloved." We must not blame the other person for our feelings. Our feelings belong to us, and usually come from what we already believe. This is how we learn to take full responsibility for our feelings and reactions toward others.

7. ASKING GOD TOUGH QUESTIONS

God, why did you allow my parents to beat me? Where were you, Lord, when my dad was molesting me? God, why did you take my child? These are typical of questions we all have. There are as many such questions as there are people. Every child of God will deal with some of them in the transforming process. Most of us have hidden places of resentment towards God. We may not want to admit them; after all, we tell ourselves, a *good Christian* wouldn't feel that way. But the truth is, we do.

It's vain to try to answer these questions out of our own intellect. Mental striving can never address the issues of the heart. The questions are directed toward God. We must not try to answer them ourselves. Sometimes people will ask me a question that is really meant for God. I never try to provide an answer. Instead, as a fellow believer, I direct them to Jesus. Only He can provide the answers that will heal our pain.

This follows my basic belief: It's better for people to hear the Lord directly than hear *me* telling them what I think He's saying. Then, the change is much more authentic and complete.

I sat with Anna as she asked God a gut-wrenching question: "Why didn't you stop me from being molested?" That's a question I never could have answered, but God spoke to her mind and heart that He was always there with her. I've shared my own experience of being molested as a child. As I dealt with that personal trauma, the Lord showed me a mental picture of Jesus covering me—while I was being molested. These intimate truths, given to us by Christ Himself, bring peace and comfort like nothing else can. I believe that Christ will always speak to us when we ask—whether we're nine or 90. God's not squeamish about hearing these tough questions. We must wait and hear from Him. Human answers won't do.

8. DEALING WITH RESISTANCE

Anyone who has counseled others knows how resistant people can be. They refuse to take responsibility for their actions. They deny their feelings. They argue. They refuse to answer questions. They transfer blame to the counselor. The only recourse in theses cases is to turn them over to God.. If someone is intent on holding onto unforgiveness and blame, I recognize my limits, and simply ask God for help. After all, I have no answers other than Christ, so I ask Him to talk with them. They may not listen, but I have removed myself from the role of rescuer, perpetrator or victim. It's always a bad sign when the counselor is doing more work than the counselee. My suggestion: take them to Christ, and let Him work.

9. WHEN TO CONFRONT

Jesus told us to go to our brother when he sins against us. If he repents, Jesus said, we have won our brother. James also tells us, ""He who turns a sinner from the error of his way will save his soul from death, and will cover a multitude of sins" (James 5:20). Sometimes, strong rebuke is called for.

So, when do we confront?

Scripture warns us to remove the beams in our own eyes before we can see clearly the speck in someone else's. All of us are deceived to some degree. This is why before confronting others we must confront our own thinking and beliefs. This is also why there is safety in a multitude of counselors. And everything said must be affirmed by the Holy Spirit. A little perspective is useful here: If I can hear and obey Jesus, why would I believe that others can't?

Paul tells us to do everything in love. That means seeking the other's best interest. We may confront, but we should never be harsh, self-righteous or condemning. The goal is to save the other from destruction, not get something we want. We confront, as the scripture says, "looking to yourselves, lest you too be tempted" (Galatians 6:1). Knowing the warning to be careful of falling into the same sin that I am judging the other for.. We may be wrong about what we observe in others. Only Jesus knows the heart. So, we should tread very lightly, and pray the Lord convicts us quickly when we mistake our judgment for His.

Again, when do we confront?" Daily—if we're talking about our own sin. If we practice that, we'll be able to hear the truth of God in our hearts. Knowing He loves us causes us to love others. And that love should guide our confronting.

10. HEAL THYSELF!

We need to trust God's work in our lives. This will help us keep on our own road of healing. Too many people in the helping professions are trying to work out their issues—by helping others. It is true that as we help others, our own issues will surface. This is where many therapists, counselors, and pastors get into trouble. They resist admitting their own vulnerabilities, thinking that will harm their credibility. But we can't lead anyone where we're unwilling to go. In fact, we cannot lead anyone where God wants them to go. Only He knows the destination He has in mind for each of His children. We must resist placing our revelation upon others. Paul warns us not to compare ourselves with others, and reminds us, "each one shall bear his own load"(Galatians 6:5).

As we recognize how much we need God's help, it will spark compassion in us for others. Paul exhorts us to "Have this attitude in yourselves which was also in Christ Jesus"(Philippians 2:5). He goes on to describe Christ's incredible humility. In the next chapter, Paul confides his own attitude of continual striving for more of Christ, saying, "Let us therefore, as many as are perfect, have this attitude; and if in anything you have a different attitude, God will reveal that also to you" (Philippians 3:15). This is how we should approach our efforts to help others.

11. DEVELOP A LIFE OF LISTENING AND CONFESSION

Listening and confessing may seem repellant at first. But it can become a lifestyle.

MAKING IT EASY: *AACT*

My clients often ask for something to help them remember the steps we go through together. Of course, this book itself is one response. But here's an acronym that summarizes the steps to wholeness: ACCT.

A—*Ask*

The Bible tells us to acknowledge God in all our ways, and not lean on our own understanding. We do that by *asking*.

What should we ask? Here are a few useful questions:

1. Lord, what do You want me to see in this situation?
2. What is really causing my pain?
3. In what areas of my life have I believed a lie?
4. What are the hidden feelings my anger is protecting me from?
5. What are the planks in my eye?
6. What is the source of my lie?
7. Where did it first take hold of me?

C—*Check*

As we review the traumatic events of our lives, we should check for the presence of resentment, vows, sin, or judgment.

A few questions can help here too:

1. Lord, is there any sin associated with this memory that I need to confess?
2. Do I have any resentment towards anyone associated with this memory?
3. Have I made any vows in response to it?
4. Have I judged anyone?

C—*Confess*

Now that we've uncovered the sin, resentment, vows, and judgment hidden in our past, we simply confess:

1. Lord, forgive me for my resentment toward _____.
2. Lord, I break the vow that I made to _____.
3. Lord, forgive me for the sin of _____.
4. Lord, forgive me for judging _____.

T—*Truth*

Having uncovered and confessed our lies, we need to hear the truth from God. This often comes when we locate the origin of the lie—the first incident that started it all. But God can speak truth at any point!

Here again, some specific petitions can help:

1. Lord, tell me the truth about my belief.
2. Where were You, Lord, when this bad thing happened to me?
3. Why did You let it happen?

Following *steps* can be risky; we tend to become religious about these things! Of course, God can address things any way He chooses, and in any sequence. But you won't go wrong by doing the things we've laid out here. Let it become a good habit! Keep asking until God answers; if the answer isn't coming, try changing the question. Trust God to direct you, and He will.

CHAPTER SEVENTEEN

Moving Forward

I have fought the good fight, I have finished the course, I have kept the faith, in the future there is laid up for me a crown of righteousness, which the Lord, the righteous judge, will award to me on that day, and not only to me, but to also all that have loved His appearing. (2 TIMOTHY 4:3)

Our very environment is designed to destroy the truth in us. How do we live then, knowing there is such deception in the world—and in us? Simply, we don't. As the apostle Paul says, "I have been crucified with Christ; and it is no longer I who live, but Christ lives in me; and the life which I now live in the flesh I live by faith in the Son of God, who loved me and gave Himself up for me" (Galatians 2:20). We should take the attitude of John the Baptist: "He must increase, but I must decrease" (John 3:30). This can only happen as we depend utterly and completely on God—and fellowship closely with our brothers and sisters in Christ. This is the essence of living.

THE COMMUNITY OF BELIEVERS

The term *community* is used in many different ways. It can refer to a neighborhood, or a group of people with common interests or characteristics. It occurs in the Bible in Exodus 12, referring to the people of Israel. For Christians, the word has nothing to do with a physical location, but denotes our kinship in Christ. This sense has largely been lost, but we are still "brethren."

Scholars tell us that in the early days of the church, there was one *community of believers* for each locality. What a joy it would be to return to that model! I fear we've lost that sense of belonging and unity within the family of God. I hope we recapture it.

Our Western culture, especially in America, is individualistic. Even in the church, it's common to hear statements such as, "If you were the only person on earth, Christ would have died for you." While this is true, and expresses how special we are to God individually, Jesus died for His beautiful *Bride*. This revelation doesn't quite fit with our individualistic ways. We tend to put our own interests before those of others. But this is not what God intended for His Bride. He wants us to love each other as Christ loves us, always placing the interests of our brothers and sisters before our own. When we begin to do this, we'll know true fellowship as God intended. This fellowship is the very thing that provides protection against the attacks of Satan. Through it we pray for one another, and enjoy the sweet, intimate fellowships of the heart.

Clearly, community is important. How do we find it?

First: find several brothers and sisters in Christ that you can confess your sin to; people who will stand with you and pray with you. To protect yourself from deception, stay in close fellowship with them, always completely dependent on Christ. Many people today ask, "Why can't I just rely on Jesus? Why do I need others?" The answer is, God designed us to need each other. And He wants us to live in unity as His Bride. We were never meant to function alone. We need each other's gifts, counsel, prayers, love, and encouragement. We also need each other's rebuke and admonition. We need the kind of love that will convict us of our sin and lead us into a closer walk with Christ. Jesus, the Head, lives and moves through His Body, and it is through the Holy Spirit that the Body functions.

Second: transformation. Jesus paid the ultimate price so we could be free. The best way to continue in this pursuit is to talk to our brothers and sisters, and have them pray for us. Often, I'll ask my wife Sandra to just listen to me as I talk about what I'm thinking and feeling. She'll ask questions to help me clarify my thoughts. As I listen to what comes out of my heart, I take note of the issues that come up. I have learned to be as honest as possible. Many times, I'll realize I'm afraid to say what I'm thinking. But learning to do that brings freedom. By exposing my heart, I experience the steps outlined in this book. It always leads to truth and freedom.

It is so important that we have someone listen to us, just for the sake of listening—without judgment or criticism. These heart-to-heart fellowships must be a safe place where trust, honesty, confidentiality, and safety are present. My prayer for all Christians is that we'll become healing listeners and prayer partners for one another.

Third: find a close fellowship of believers who are totally and utterly dependent on Christ and who listen to the voice of the Holy Spirit. In the book of Acts we read that the early believers were "breaking bread from house to house" (Acts 2:46). This constant gathering and celebration of Christ fostered intimate, heart-to-heart relationships. How can we know true fellowship if we never spend enough time with each other to expose our hearts? We need a place where we can be transparent with each other, and also confront each other in love. When we confront others, we often find out more about ourselves than the other person. That's why we must be willing to expose our hearts.

It is critical that we align ourselves with those who are walking in the truth; who will encourage us to turn from sin, experience our pain, and seek God. It is always a miraculous experience to stand with a friend in prayer, and witness firsthand the power of Jesus as He sets them free. To rejoice and cry alongside our brothers and sisters, celebrating each victory, big or small; to see the glory of God manifest as they express the Kingdom of God—that is community

Many people today endorse home churches as the best way to experience intimate fellowship. My only prayer is that wherever God leads you, you'll find people who are living life together and are accountable to one another. This requires experiencing life together beyond the church walls. To grow and mature in our Christian walk, we need brothers and sisters who will mentor and pray for us. It is in seeking Christ together, and praying for one another, that we cultivate intimate heart-to-heart fellowships.

EMBRACE THE WORD

Many times, I've witnessed firsthand the power of the Word of God to heal and transform believers. When Jesus was tested by Satan in the desert, He responded to each temptation with, "It is written ..." He never argued with Satan or tried to persuade. He simply quoted the word of God. These same words today, immortalized in scripture, have the power to overcome the power of Satan and set the captives free.

Sometimes, the Holy Spirit directs me to read a passage of the Bible to people, addressing them personally by name. It is wondrous to witness Him delivering and setting them free. We must never forget that the word of God is the sword of the Spirit (Ephesians 6:17). While some parts of the church focus on our spiritual gifts, they forget that the greatest weapon has already been given to us. The word of God is powerful (Hebrews 4:12). It must not only be taught, but believed and acted upon. This is especially important in resolving the pain and problems in our life. We must make absolutely certain that the community we seek is the community of Christ. Seek fellowship, study the word of God, and listen to the voice of your Savior, the living and true Word, each and every day. He alone is life. Do not be afraid that you won't hear Him when you call. God watches over His word to perform it. You will hear His voice (John 10:27). Trust his word. It will keep you in the way of transformation.

And never forget that the blood of Jesus cleanses us from all our sin. How? *Confession. confession. confession.*

PRACTICE MAKES PERFECT

Learning the ways of God is not an easy task. We are constantly at war with our old nature. And years of deception may take more than a few days to overcome. Each one of us was born into deception and sin. Most of us have spent our lives protecting ourselves, eating from the tree of the knowledge of good and evil. This will leave long-lasting effects. Be patient with yourself!

Also, as you learn and grow in community, be patient with others. God tells us His heart so clearly: "I desire mercy, not sacrifice" (Matthew 9:13).

Practice showing mercy to one another. Always remember that "love covers a multitude of sins" (1 Peter 4:8). Experiencing the new life will not be fast or easy. But it will be simple: We lay down what we want for what Christ wants. And when we submit to the work of the Holy Spirit in us, God is faithful to work these things in us. Jesus is always working in us to will and to do of His good pleasure (Philippians 2:13). It is His faith working in us to bring us to completion.

As you begin to practice the principles outlined in this book, something spectacular will happen. You'll become more aware of the words you speak. The issues of your heart will be revealed to you. You'll find that as you confess your sins more and more, it becomes second nature. You'll enjoy the freedom that comes from exposing your heart to your brothers and sisters and confessing your sin. You will find heart-to-heart relationships developing on their own, for the sake of Christ, and not of your own doing. Continue to pursue the kingdom and ask God daily to show you the issues in your heart. He is faithful and true to answer you when you call.

A FINAL WORD

Practice, practice, practice the tools provided in this book. Do the ACCT steps continually. Ask, check, confess and talk to God in everything. Acknowledge Him, Don't believe what you believe. Don't lean on your own understanding. He will direct you.

If you're a minister, counselor or group leader, you will find that the biblical principles outlined in this book can expedite the deliverance, counseling, healing, and comforting process. But a quick word of caution: While these are practical tools for healing, we must always be dependent on the Holy Spirit for discernment and direction. This dependency requires patience, and comes with maturity in Christ.

Surround yourself with brothers and sisters in Christ and *meet* together often, so that Christ-centered relationships can flourish. We need these relationships, not merely acquaintances, so we can confess our sins to one another (James 5:16), expose our hearts, and pray for one another. In these relationships, we learn how to listen to God's voice corporately, submit to one another, and walk together in unity. They mirror the type of relationship Jesus had with His disciples, and they are what He always intended for us. *Seek* mentors and counselors who have walked ahead of you and who are worthy of their calling—broken men and women who walk closely with God and are completely dependent on Him. In that brokenness, you will find brothers and sisters of the faith who possess the jewels that come from years of experience; who have endured the painful crushing and pruning seasons of life. It is these men and women of the faith who have walked the long, uphill path, from Gethsemane to Calvary, crucified their flesh, and been resurrected with a new understanding of the mercy, grace, authority, power and truth of God.

Do not be afraid. Perfect love casts all out fear. God is for you, not against you. When you call on the name of the Lord, He will save and deliver you. Start to speak with Him daily. If you don't have a relationship with Him at all, invite Jesus into your heart. Remember, it is always those simple, child-like conversations that God cherishes most. Begin to speak to Him, and learn to listen quietly, and you will hear His still small voice. God will never disappoint you. He may delay, just as He did with Lazarus, but He will never disappoint. God will never leave you and He will never forsake you. Most importantly, God loves you, and it is this love, expressed by Him and through His people, that transforms.

Finally, *never forget* this important Truth: Jesus paid the ultimate price, death on a cross, for you to be *free*! Jesus destroyed and completely obliterated the works of the enemy and overcame death. That authority and power sets us free today. Submit yourself to God and resist the enemy. Confess your sin. Ask for forgiveness. When we turn our hearts to God, He is faithful to deliver, heal, and restore His children (2 Chronicles 7:14; Matthew 15:26).

And always remember—Love *never* fails!

**

INDEX

A

addictions, 2, 33, 34, 112, 137, 138
agape, 7, 31, 32

C

confess, 6, 11, 21, 25, 27, 28, 32, 38, 40, 41, 52, 65, 66, 69, 74, 77, 83, 85, 87, 89, 92, 93, 95, 98, 100, 102, 111, 112, 113, 114, 120, 121, 127, 126, 128, 130, 131, 133, 134, 135, 136, 137, 138, 139, 140, 145, 146, 147, 148, 150, 151, 155, 156, 162, 163, 164

D

deception, 3, 6, 9, 11, 12, 13, 14, 15, 17, 18, 20, 21, 23, 25, 27, 30, 32, 41, 44, 62, 65, 67, 68, 69, 73, 75, 76, 77, 79, 90, 96, 101, 108, 109, 112, 123, 125, 126, 127, 128, 130, 133, 134, 136, 138, 139, 142, 145, 147, 159, 160, 162

E

enemy, 2, 11, 15, 16, 17, 18, 20, 21, 23, 25, 34, 37, 70, 71, 73, 79, 112, 113, 124, 130, 135, 136, 139, 164

F

forgiveness, 6, 21, 25, 44, 52, 57, 75, 77, 82, 83, 84, 85, 86, 87, 88, 90, 99, 100, 102, 114, 134, 138, 138, 147, 151, 153
freedom, 1, 2, 28, 42, 73, 74, 88, 90, 94, 95, 96, 101, 102, 121, 123, 137, 148, 152, 161

H

healing, 1, 2, 4, 9, 11, 13, 15, 17, 18, 19, 20, 21, 25, 26, 27, 28, 29, 33, 35, 36, 37, 38, 39, 40, 41, 42, 42, 43, 44, 45, 46, 47, 48, 49, 50, 53, 56, 65, 66, 76, 84, 86, 88, 92, 98, 99, 100, 102, 108, 109. 110, 123, 124, 125, 126, 127, 129, 130, 131, 133, 134, 135, 136, 137, 139, 141, 142, 143, 148, 149, 151, 152, 153 155, 161, 162, 163

I

image, 4, 6, 10, 11, 12, 13, 14, 15, 16, 17, 18, 19, 24, 26, 30, 31, 32, 36, 37, 38, 44, 49, 62, 66, 68, 71, 72, 75, 84, 86, 88, 90, 103, 129, 130, 134, 135

J

judgment, 51, 53, 73 , 75, 77, 78, 88, 92, 95, 97, 98, 99, 100, 101, 102, 103, 118, 124, 125, 136, 139, 140, 141, 142, 151, 154, 156, 161

L

lies, 11, 12, 15, 17, 20, 27, 29, 33, 38, 41, 44, 51, 53, 55, 57, 59, 60, 61, 62, 63, 64, 65, 66, 67, 68, 69, 75, 76, 79, 83, 85, 84, 87, 86, 88, 91, 98, 99, 107, 108, 112, 127, 129, 134, 136, 138, 141, 142, 151, 150, 156

love, 3, 5, 12, 16, 19, 20, 25, 27, 28, 31, 34, 39, 42, 44, 47, 48, 50, 53, 54, 57, 62, 64, 66, 68, 69, 73, 74, 76, 79, 82, 90, 93, 99, 106, 107, 108, 109, 111, 110, 112, 118, 119, 120, 122, 125, 129, 136, 138, 145 146, 147, 149, 150, 151, 154, 159, 160, 164

M

marriage, 4, 5, 30, 39, 50, 51, 60, 78, 93, 94, 101, 102, 112, 118, 119, 120, 147

mature-minded, 143

O

obey, 12, 16, 27, 28, 54, 78, 97, 98, 127, 128, 154

P

pain, 1, 3, 5, 6, 11, 12, 15, 18, 19, 31, 33, 37, 38, 39, 40, 42, 43, 44, 47, 48, 49, 50, 51, 52, 53, 54, 55, 56, 57, 59, 60, 61, 62, 64, 66, 69, 73, 74, 75, 76, 79, 81, 82, 83, 84, 86, 87, 89, 90, 92, 93, 94, 96, 98, 99, 100, 102, 106, 107, 108, 110, 112, 113, 114, 116, 118, 119, 120, 126, 128, 129, 131, 133, 134, 136, 138, 139, 1421 143, 147, 149, 150, 151, 152, 153, 156, 161, 162, 164

psychology, 2, 3, 6, 78, 99, 125, 129

R

redemption, 16, 30

resentment, 4, 5, 51, 53, 56, 73, 75, 77, 78, 81, 82, 83, 84, 85, 86, 87, 88, 90, 91, 92, 95, 98, 99, 100, 102, 106, 111, 114, 121, 138, 139, 140, 145, 146, 151, 152, 153, 156

S

sin, 1, 2, 3, 6, 11, 12, 14, 15, 16, 18, 19, 20, 21, 23, 24, 25, 26, 27, 28, 32, 33, 34, 35, 36, 37, 38, 40, 41, 44, 49, 51, 52, 54, 55, 56, 57, 59, 60, 65, 66, 67, 68, 69, 72, 73, 74, 75, 76, 77, 82, 83, 84, 88, 87, 89, 90, 91, 92, 95, 96, 99, 100, 101, 102, 108, 109, 111, 112, 113, 114, 116, 118, 119, 120, 121, 124, 125, 126, 127, 128, 129, 130, 131, 133, 134, 135, 136, 137, 138, 139, 140, 141, 145, 146, 147, 149, 150, 154, 156, 160, 161, 162, 163, 164

strongholds, 4, 5, 15, 20, 28, 31, 32, 40, 41, 42, 43, 44, 45, 51, 54, 69, 71, 72, 73, 74, 75, 76, 77, 78, 79, 83, 85, 88, 92, 98, 99, 102, 108, 127, 130, 135, 141, 150, 152

T

transformation, 1, 3, 9, 20, 25, 26, 27, 28, 35, 36, 41, 42, 50, 60, 69, 92, 110, 111, 112, 127, 134, 135, 136, 139, 148, 149, 160, 162

U

unforgiveness, 6, 52, 73, 75, 77, 82, 83, 84, 86, 87, 88, 90, 136, 151, 153

V

vows, 4, 38, 51, 53, 73, 75, 77, 78 86, 89, 90, 91, 92, 93, 94, 95, 96, 111, 136, 139, 140, 141, 143, 151, 156

W

wife, 6, 7, 24, 32, 40, 50, 54, 58, 63, 64, 66, 82, 97, 100, 101, 109, 110, 128, 131, 133, 150, 167, 174

Made in the USA
Columbia, SC
13 April 2021